POETRY MATTERS

Edited by Vivien Linton

Nottinghamshire & Derbyshire

First published in Great Britain in 2011 by:

Young Writers

Remus House
Coltsfoot Drive
Peterborough
PE2 9BF
Telephone: 01733 890066
Website: www.youngwriters.co.uk

Foreword

Since our inception in 1991, Young Writers has endeavoured to promote poetry and creative writing within schools by running annual nationwide competitions. These competitions are designed to develop and nurture the burgeoning creativity of the next generation, and give them valuable confidence in their own abilities.

This regional anthology is one of the series produced by our latest secondary school competition, *Poetry Matters*. Using poetry as their tool, the young writers were given the opportunity to tell the world what matters to them. The authors of our favourite three poems were also given the chance to appear on the front cover of their region's collection.

Whilst skilfully conveying their opinions through poetry, the writers showcased in this collection have simultaneously managed to give poetry a breath of fresh air, brought it to life and made it relevant to them. Using a variety of themes and styles, our featured poets leave a lasting impression of their inner thoughts and feelings, making this anthology a rare insight into the next generation.

Contents

Eastwood Comprehensive School, Nottingham

Hollygirt School, Nottingham

Manning School for Girls, Aspley

Portland Comprehensive School, Worksop

Royal School for the Deaf, Derby

St John Houghton Catholic School, Kirk Hallam

Wilsthorpe Community School, Long Eaton

The Poems

My Guitar

Strumming through the day, all day, every day.
Holding notes, changing notes
Strumming through the day
Putting notes together
Strumming through the day.

Strumming through the day, all day every day.
Making songs, singing songs
Strumming through the day
Writing notes down
Strumming through the day.

Strumming through the day, all day every day.
Singing about life, singing about death
Strumming through the day
Watching the world go by
Strumming through the day.

Strumming through the day, all day every day.
Singing about that girl, singing about the one
Strumming through the day
Singing about the future, singing about the past
Strumming through the day.

Strumming through the day, all day every day.
Forget about sleeping, forget about eating
Strumming through the day.

Edward Faulkner (12)
Bennerley Business & Enterprise College, Ilkeston

My Dog, Jasper

My dog, my dog, I love him lots,
His name is Jasper.
His nose is big and black
And his fur's as white as snow.
I throw his toy carrot
Then he'll go and bring it back.
He likes to wave goodbye to you
And even have a chat with you.
'Walkies,' I say as his tail wags fast
And his ears prick up in excitement.
He loves his food from biscuits to bones,
But the one thing he won't eat - carrots.
My dog, my dog is very clever
And I love him so very much.

Ashleigh Sutton (13)
Bennerley Business & Enterprise College, Ilkeston

Friends And Family

Life can be a downer,
But have upsides too,
But the thing that matters most of all is friends and family.
My big bro I think he should wear a bow,
Also my little bro is the star of the show,
And my mum and dad are pro.
Now to my friends,
Who can drive you around the bend,
I first start with Rob, he always has a job,
Next comes Kristen,
He can break your piston,
Next Emma, but there's nothing to rhyme with that!
Last there's Megan but let's just call her a pelican
Because she watched over us all.

Elliot Mills
Bennerley Business & Enterprise College, Ilkeston

Metal Music

Banging those sticks on that drum,
Sounding like a man on the run,
Plucking that string, filling the room,
Waking up ancient mummies from buried tombs.

Performing for us, brilliant all the time,
People pay their money, every last dime,
They always sound good, every last song,
Succeeding always, never going wrong.

Whenever we play, they call us kings,
Gold or diamond are all of our rings,
Brought from the money, that we all earn,
Never called rubbish, we would be concerned.

When we play, the stage is lit with fire,
Wanting our songs, that's all they desire,
In thousands of years, people will tell,
Of nights we destroyed minds, creating hell.

Jeremy Krakowiak [12]
Bennerley Business & Enterprise College, Ilkeston

Heroes

The trigger of a gun.
The braveness of a soldier.
The life of a loved one.

The mums, the sons.
The fathers, the brothers.
That went to war for us.

They risk their lives for us.
That's what matters to me.
That's what matters to me.

Emma Ashley [12]
Bennerley Business & Enterprise College, Ilkeston

What Matters To Me

At first I'll talk about football,
We play on a field and against a wall;
I support Notts County, whilst eating a Bounty
Play for Stanton, the pressure's mountin'

Then onto family, my dad he is the leader;
My mum is very caring, but I hate what she is wearing;
My brother is a nutter, he likes to be a fairy and flutter.

I also have two pets,
Both cats, but not with hats;
Nearly forgot the fish,
Jess, Messi and Tom; they like to watch Gok Wan.

Next I'll talk about food;
My favourite is Italian,
Eaten by the first battalion.
It is spaghetti Bolognese,
Hold the mayonnaise.

They are the things that matter to me,
Until next time,
Goodbyeeeeeee!

Kieran Widdowson (13)
Bennerley Business & Enterprise College, Ilkeston

The Photo On The Wall

We sit and wait,
For the phone to ring,
Before it's too late,
We hear a ding.

We run to the door,
Hoping it's him,
We run on the floor,
And let the man in.

He walks in smartly,
He smiles weakly,
He speaks sharply,
He looks sleekly.

He says, 'Sit down,'
We say, 'No,'
He says he's sorry,
Then we cry, 'No!'

My mum sits down,
With a bit of a fall,
Will we always remember
The photo on the wall?

Dylan Booth
Bennerley Business & Enterprise College, Ilkeston

The Roller Coaster Of My Life

Life is a roller coaster
It goes round and round.
My behaviour as a child
Had its ups and downs.

As my brother turns on the Xbox,
I quickly put him in a headlock.
As I go out to play football,
My mum has a go because I hit the shed door.

I tell my mum I want a pet
But my mum says, 'No! Not yet.'
On a Thursday I have karate,
It is definitely not a party.

On Tuesday I play football
But sometimes I'm just dull and bored.
Most of the time I am cheeky,
And all of the time I am naughty.

Joe Jameson
Bennerley Business & Enterprise College, Ilkeston

What Matters To Me

What matters to me.
My mum, dad, brother, nana, grandad are glad to be part of my family.
Always taking care of each other, helping one another.
Going on holiday with friends in the sun, playing games and having fun.
My brother's on the attack on 'Fifa 11'
He has shot and I block it with a diving header.
I'm in a shot-put competition.
Throwing for the team and I throw a seven.
On the TV there is Formula 1. 1 light, 2, 3 lights, 4,
One more and the 5 go out, there's a roar and it's go, go, go.
My favourite hobby is 'Halo Reach'.
Playing the Xbox 360,
Shootin' and lootin' people around the world,
Stealing flags and taking skulls.
This is what matters to me.

Aaron Trueman (12)
Bennerley Business & Enterprise College, Ilkeston

Music Matters To Us

As soon as we walk through the door,
We go upstairs, we can't take it anymore,
We go to our room,
And start punching a big balloon.
But as soon as the songs come on,
Our anger has completely gone.
We start dancing around,
So we look like a clown.
But we don't care anymore, about anyone!
So then our fave song is on,
Our happiness has completely gone.
We start skipping around, we have butterflies now,
Because Bruno Mars is on!

Emma Gilbert & Mia Locke
Bennerley Business & Enterprise College, Ilkeston

Football Players Poem

Lionel Messi with his skills,
Frank Lampard's goal clearly hit the net,
Aaron Ramsey with his broken leg,
Ryan Shawcross sees red,
Cesc Fabregas showing the tricks,
Didier Drogba can't stop scoring,
Wayne Rooney is just boring,
David Villa is the best,
Joe Hart flying here and there,
Aaron Lennon down the wing,
Kaka the Brazilian mastermind,
Cristiano Ronaldo chucking himself on the floor every time you blink,
He even gives you a special wink,
And that's why football matters to me.

Cieran Boot (12)
Bennerley Business & Enterprise College, Ilkeston

My New Dog!

My new doggy loves to play
Night and also day
He is a very white dog
And also he's a sofa hog
He has two black circles around his eyes
And he's a really big fan of apple pies!
My dog is very cuddly
And he has a name, it's Dudley
My dog is very wild
He is like a 2-year-old child
I know he wants to sleep in my bed
But he's not allowed because my mum said
I'd love to take Dudley with me to school
All my friends would love him because he is
So cool!

Ellie Johnson (11)
Bennerley Business & Enterprise College, Ilkeston

Animals

Animals are great, especially pets.
Unfortunately sometimes they need to visit the vets.
My dog whimpers like a crying baby
She shakes and she shivers but it's a yes not a maybe.
An injection of medicine to stop dog disease
Soon it's all over then she's as happy as a swarm of buzzing bees.
We soon zoom back home and she flies to her bed
Fast asleep, all snuggled like a baby just fed.

Chloe Peace (11)
Dronfield Henry Fanshawe School, Dronfield

Animals

My cat, my cat, is ever so fat.
He eats more than he should.
He cannot run but he could.
And he rolls in sloppy mud.
My cat has a girlfriend but he is as filthy as a hobo.
I'd like a snack because she can crush my brother as easy as a pie.
I'd like a snack.
It would be cool if it could swim in a pool.
I would like a snack because it would be cool.

Nathan Jones (11)
Dronfield Henry Fanshawe School, Dronfield

Sport

Sport is exciting,
Entertaining, enjoyable,
Sport is interesting,
Fun, passionate

I play a lot of tennis,
But not in Venice,
At Graves instead,
I keep my racket in the shed.

I like watching football,
When the referees fall,
It makes me laugh,
Because they are daft.

I also watch cricket,
And when they take a wicket,
I groan or cheer,
So that everyone can hear.

James Naylor (12)
Dronfield Henry Fanshawe School, Dronfield

A Job At Moorview

Every weekend I work at Moorview Golf Centre.
Then I go and collect the balls off the range field.
Then I drive the tractor on the par 3 course which has a door of a metal shield.
After the collection we wash them in the washer.
This sometimes acts like a dosser.
Then we get our dosh.
With the money I look posh.
Then we go home to get prepared for another 6am wake up,
so we can go to work again.

Tom Bates [14]
Dronfield Henry Fanshawe School, Dronfield

Music Poem

When I'm feeling down,
I go upstairs I place the earphones on my head,
And then the world stands still.
Then my face fades from red.

But there's still a storm in my brain,
I know it's all in my mind,
But now the anger's beginning to drain,
I'm also beginning to find,
That I love music and that's final.

I find that rock clears my head,
Better than the rest
I need it like a duck needs bread
It opens my head like a pirate chest.

Richard Hebblethwaite [12]
Dronfield Henry Fanshawe School, Dronfield

PS3

The PS3 is for me,
There's nothing that I like more
It doesn't anger, it doesn't bore
The temptation I can't ignore.
My favourite is 'Call of Duty'
'COD', for short
That one I gladly claim to have bought.
Films, music, games and more you can do.
Why people think Xbox is better
I do not have a clue.
It is quite obvious PS3 is the console of choice
With its free internet and better service
You cannot diss.
My point you cannot miss
'Cause it's right there in writing
Xbox lovers,
There's no point in fighting
If I'm wrong strike me with lightning . . .
Ha!

Oliver Wilson (12)
Dronfield Henry Fanshawe School, Dronfield

Call Of Duty 6

'Call of Duty'
A game that's cool
If you hate it
You're a fool
It's a game that kicks ass
Get a nuke
Kill everything
AC-130
Turns everything dirty
AK-47
Kills
And sends them up into Heaven
Riot shield
Bulletproof
Stops an idiot shooting you
It's extreme
Killing an opponent
And them falling in the stream
Whoop, whoop
Whoop, whoop.

Harrison Walker (12)
Dronfield Henry Fanshawe School, Dronfield

Halloween

Halloween o Halloween
Hear the little children scream
Children go out to trick or treat
Begging people for some sweets
Witches scream and crackle in the night
But by then I am tucked in bed tight
The skeletons and their thin white bones
Wobble about on rocks and stones
The zombies do their monthly dance
Even the dead join in with the prance
The ones buried on the ground
Come alive and make frightful sounds
Children go out with their friends
Hoping the witching hour never ends!

Grace Bond (12)
Dronfield Henry Fanshawe School, Dronfield

A Poem About Swimming With My Friends

I go to the changing rooms
Come out in my dazzling swimming costume
I go splash!
Jumping into the sparkling pool
Getting all my friends more and more cool.
They go, 'Emma why do you always have to go that far?'
I get back out the pool going
Drip, drip, drip onto the very slippery floor.
I nearly slip but then I suddenly
Splash back into the pool.
I spring back to the top as I gasp for some air.

Emma Peace (11)
Dronfield Henry Fanshawe School, Dronfield

Halloween

The pumpkin at my table
Keeps on smiling more and more
There's a ghost who haunts my bedroom,
A witch on her broom
Flying by my window,
A spider crawling by my feet.
So now I know it's Halloween
It's time to go and trick or treat.

Elle-May Allsop (12)
Dronfield Henry Fanshawe School, Dronfield

My Friends . . .

My friends always make me happy,
Memories I'll never ever lose,
And they never fail to amuse,
They'll never leave my heart.

We'll always be there through thick and thin,
Loads of fun times together we have had,
To have such good friends makes me so glad,
We shop, party and just muck about

Helping each other when we're sometimes down,
They're supporting no matter what life throws,
When with them my heart positively glows
I love them so much I'll never forget.

The word loves means everything,
That is why I'll always love them,
Because they mean everything to me.

Alicia Charles (13)
Dronfield Henry Fanshawe School, Dronfield

Everything . . .

My family and friend mean everything to me.
They care for me when I feel sad.
I love them more than the next-door neighbour's lad.
Izzy, Rose and Katie are cooler than cool.
They are not as boring as a fool.
We always fight, but make up in the end,
But sometimes they can drive me around the bend.
So what can I say about Elise and Ellie?
All these years we have been good mates.
Since we met each other at the school gates.
From Reception to Year 6 and now into Fanshawe.
We seem closer than ever more.
Secrets we all share but never to be told.
That our hearts will forever hold.
Forever friends I hope we stay.
For all the years that come and go away.
So in a few or many years.
Let's hope there are not a lot of tears.
Just think of all the happy memories we have shared over the years.

Libby Jones (12)
Dronfield Henry Fanshawe School, Dronfield

Unsocial Network

I'll see what you've been up to,
In a place where time suspends,
Hung up on walls for me to view,
What's up with all my friends,

Friends I haven't spoken to
For forever and a day
Or friends I've never met who
I added anyway

A comment on my wall, a link
Perhaps a status update.
As powerful as a strong drink
It keeps you up till late.

Before I click to view your photos
And all your conversations.
Perhaps you didn't know that those
Were public complications

Some use it to keep in touch
Some use it to find a wife
Others use it far too much
But remember, you've still got a life.

Abby Booker (12)
Dronfield Henry Fanshawe School, Dronfield

Fingers

I have 10 fingers
2 of them are thumbs
They help me to write and draw
I wish I had more
They help me to pick things up
Such as a cup
They help me to drive a car
Otherwise I wouldn't get far
That's how I get to the bar
That's when I got drunk
Someone stole my purse and I shouted,
'You little punk!'
That's when my heart sunk
I realised my car keys were in there
That's so unfair
So I walked home
And I fell over
I drank a cup of coffee
That's how I got sober
So without fingers or thumbs
You couldn't work out sums
And school would be over.

Lauren Hartley & Emma Tyler (13)
Dronfield Henry Fanshawe School, Dronfield

A Billion Dollars

My dream, in my own words I guess,
I know that,
Everybody has a similar sort of dream but,
I wanna hold my wallet in the air and shout out,
I want a billion dollars and a Bentley in my driveway,
If it happens I'll be doing it my way,
With Brad and Angelina in my house yeah,
Giving birth to a ton o babies they ain't never had yet,
That's sick Brad,
Holly crap man! Why you playing with that thang?
Damn!
I'd be playing basketball with the president,
Tiger Woods 'n' Michael Jordan getting their ass whooped
Hey Mr President, winnin's as sweet as a how
How,
Innit!
Obama, you wouldn't understand,
I'm gonna drink a martini with Bill Gates now man,
Oh! I'm goin mad over . . .
A billion dollars and a Bentley in my driveway
Our dreams will never die,
In our heart and in our minds,
I'd be rappin away,
All day, every day,
For the new blockbuster with Ralph Fiennes,
What would you do?

John Reaney (12)
Dronfield Henry Fanshawe School, Dronfield

Hollister

I stop and stare,
This is when I enter,
Everything's fabtastic,
Wow! A designer hoodie in the centre,

At first I thought it was a restaurant,
Now it's a miracle,
So trendy and grand,
It's just so beautiful,

Cool! Awesome up to date clothes,
They fulfil all your dreams,
Colourful, designer and quite sporty,
Every girl's heart will be filled with glee!

It's dark and it's groovy,
It's where I like to shop,
I could shop in there forever,
And shop till I drop!

Loads of lipgloss!
Fresh mango, wild berry, mint frost,
I love many things in here,
Oh, but look at the cost!

Just when I think it couldn't get any better . . .
What a scent!
Strawberries and rose petals,
Lovely smell of perfume everywhere I went!

So girly . . . I need it!
Such a fab dress,
Awww! I don't have any cash left,
I'm in a mess!

It's closed!
How terribly tragic,
Many fashionable surroundings still un-seen,
Hollister is immensely magic!

Mary Saxton [12]
Dronfield Henry Fanshawe School, Dronfield

Tough Love

I love to watch you,
When you're around,
'Cause my feet are by the ceiling,
And my head is on the ground,
I think it's called love,
I'll have to tough it through,
But I can't see the bad side of you,
With the halo above,
Your head.

Lucy Whelan (12)
Dronfield Henry Fanshawe School, Dronfield

Music!

I like rap
Cos it makes my foot tap, tap, tap

I like hip hop
Makes the beat drop, drop, drop

MJ he was the best
He was better than the rest

I think jazz is cool
But you may think it is drool

I don't care what you think 'bout this song
You may think I'm very wrong

But this is me I like this stuff
And yeah maybe I ain't so tough

Music makes me feel happy
Some songs can be very snappy

Boo yah!

Ben Davy (12)
Dronfield Henry Fanshawe School, Dronfield

I Do Not Want To Go To Bed

I do not want to go to bed
I like to stay up late.
I'm bouncing off the bedroom walls
and, frankly, feeling great!

I'm dancing like a maniac
instead of counting sheep.
My mom says, 'Time for bed.'
My dad yells, 'Get your butt to sleep!'

I'm not sure what my bottom
has to do with anything,
but that's okay because I'd rather
jump around and sing.

I don't know what it was
that made me feel so wide awake.
Could it have been the Red Bull
and the double-chocolate cake?

I wonder if the seven cups
of coffee plus dessert
of Hershey bars and Skittles
are what left me this alert?

Whatever it turns out to be
that made me feel this right,
I hope I track it down
so I can stay up every . . . zzzzzzzz.

Harry Browes (13)
Dronfield Henry Fanshawe School, Dronfield

Sheffield Wednesday

I like football
And I support Wednesday
I go every week
But we play on Saturday! Not Wednesday.

They play in blue and white
And they keep me up at night
But I'm not bothered
Because I have a nightlight! I don't really.

They play at Hillsborough
But not against Middlesbrough
Because they're in the league above
But when push comes to shove . . .
We're better than them anyway!

We're known as the owls
We don't commit a lot of fouls
We're on the prowl
To win the next game . . . Against Bournemouth.

Whilst we're in 4th place
Richard plays his bass
We'll be top soon
But not before noon!

We've got a great keeper
And he's called Nicky Weaver
He saves a load of penalties
Ha-ha, Chesterfield!

William Newton (13)
Dronfield Henry Fanshawe School, Dronfield

Art Poem

Art is in my heart,
art is in my blood,
I do it every day,
drawing everyday life.

The scratch of pencil on paper,
the image now forming,
lots of vivid colours,
the soft brush of paint,
the watercolours blending together,
as a masterpiece of art is made.

The bright colourful crayons
blending together,
making a colourful picture,
the bright white-coloured chalk,
the ideas forming,
highlighting the picture.

Amazement of what has formed,
hanging on the wall,
eyes turned,
from me,
to the wall,
to my pictures.

Laura Welsby (13)
Dronfield Henry Fanshawe School, Dronfield

Unseen Heroes

The sound of a jeep
a knock on the door
I know that he must go once more
off to Afghanistan
with all of his troops
each one of them brave and loyal recruits
tears in my eyes
a kiss on the cheek
don't worry my darling all will be sweet
a letter sent
a letter returned
each one with a kiss and
new things to be learned
the sound of a jeep
a knock on the door
I know that he is home once more
but to my surprise an officer's here
who tells me news I don't
want to hear
a tear rolls down my pale white face
as I take a moment to
remember your face.

Millie McVay (13)
Dronfield Henry Fanshawe School, Dronfield

The Olympic Games!

As the fire is lit, the games begin
Running, swimming and gymnastics
They are the best
Running like lightning, lightning
Or running for miles and miles
Swimming fast or slow
Diving high and long
Twisting and turning from the biggest board
Pushing off from tumble turns
Fastest start from the block
Tumbling, turning and spinning
Flying off the vault
Swinging higher, higher over the asymmetric bars
Balancing and posing on the beam
Crowds clapping
Judges judging
Medal awarded to first, second and third.
I would love to go to the Olympics
Wouldn't you?

Elise Dawson (12)
Dronfield Henry Fanshawe School, Dronfield

A Legend To Be

I pull my leg back to smash the ball
To find out I've gone and scored a goal
The roaring fans chant my name
Well, I've just run the game.

Done, the game has ended
Well, my goal was splendid
Yes, I won the game
At least this time I'm not to blame.

Wow! The mad fans run on
For the first time I thought I shone
The excited fans leap on me
They showed that I'm a legend to be.

Finally, I struggled my way through
At first, I don't know what to do
The tunnel I run
To get a praise for what I've done.

This is a dream that won't come true
No matter what I do
A legend to be?
That won't be me.

Charlie Glossop (13)
Dronfield Henry Fanshawe School, Dronfield

My Elephant Dream

I was once in the zoo,
When I smelt some poo,
I walked towards the scent,
When I saw an elephant,
The elephant moved as its feet went thud!
Then he walked towards a puddle of mud,
He sat in it splash, as the mud went all over,
Then he looked at me and I nearly fell over,
Suddenly he made a choo with his trunk,
That's when I woke up and I'm lying in my bed bunk!

April Stocks (11)
Dronfield Henry Fanshawe School, Dronfield

Love Sonnet

Thy love for you is strong and true,
For this I declare my love to you:
Although nothing can compare,
In my heart, you're always there.
Eternal love will never fade,
Till our last breathe has gone.
And these eyes no longer see,
Let your love belong to thee.
But unfortunately life is harsh,
And soon our lives will end.
But until that day,
When we lay,
There is something you should know.
I love you lots and will forever,
And hope that we stay together.

Devon Leaper (14)
Dronfield Henry Fanshawe School, Dronfield

What's The News? New Shoes?

Shoes, shoes, shoes
Red, pink and blue . . .
What's new with the news?
I have some new shoes!

Shoes I need you . . .
Like bananas and custard.
Even like hotdogs and mustard.
Custard, mustard, whatever you are
Shoes you're just like my star.

Dancing shoes, prancing shoes,
Trendy and cool shoes,
Any colour of the neon rainbow shoes.
Rainbow, raving, respect . . .
These ain't no shoes to mess with!

Walk into my house - walk into my house . . .
And you will see . . .
I can guarantee . . .
No mouse.
But something you will see
Is shoes
Shoes, shoes, everywhere
Even in my hair!

These feet huggers,
Ain't no muggers,
Because these are shoes,
That put me outta my blues.

Eleanor Bell (12)
Dronfield Henry Fanshawe School, Dronfield

Team Deathmatch On Modern Warfare 2

Shotgun shells and sniper ammo,
Riot shields and arctic camo.

I'll stab you with my knife,
I'll snipe you with my barrett.

Predator Drone is online!

Everyone's killin' on 'Modern Warfare 2',
I'll call in my chopper gunner,
And it's comin' for you!

I'm gonna catch you dirty with my AC-130!

Runnin round the corner with my UMP,
Just killed a camper which makes me happy!

Just got a 360,
What a great fluke!
Time to end the game with a tactical nuke!

Thomas Woolley, Jordan M Parry, Harry Browes & Harry Bingham (13)
Dronfield Henry Fanshawe School, Dronfield

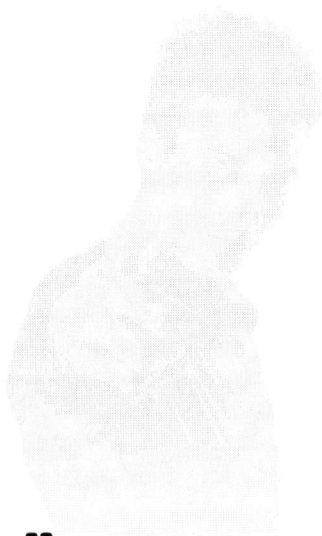

Art

I wait all day
For that one hour
A lesson that I love

It's in my heart
It's in my blood
It's what I really love

The soft brush on the paper
The pencils gentle scratch
The dust from the chalk
The oil pastel's wax

The crayons blending colours
The charcoal ink black
The bright red felt-tip
The paper's sharp cut

I wait all day
For that one hour
A lesson that I love

It's in my heart
It's in my blood
It's what I really love.

Elizabeth Wilson (13)
Dronfield Henry Fanshawe School, Dronfield

Friendship Matters To Me

What matters to me is my friends,
Because friendship is something that never ends.
When I am down they pick me up,
When I am nervous they give me luck,
When I need help they are always there,
All of my secrets with them I can share.

Without them a party would never be the same,
I would have no one to dance with which would be a shame.
We're the ones partying all night long,
Singing along to our favourite song,
Dancing to the beat of 'Dynamite'
Waving our hands in the air all through the night.

When we are walking around Meadowhall,
Without our parents, feeling fifty foot tall.
Sipping smoothies and carrying heavy bags,
Giggling as we gaze at the good looking lads,
Running through shops so we don't miss the train,
Checking the train times, yet again!

My friends are so important to me,
The ones who make me laugh hysterically.
My friends are the people who are always there,
The people I know who'll always care.
My love for my friends is like no other
Not like I love my parents and love my brother.
I love my family so very much
But my friends have something just as precious.
They feel like my sisters who I can always trust,
If I make a mistake they are not fussed,
My friends make me who I am,
I love them, I need them, I'm their number one fan!

Eleanor Thomas (12)
Dronfield Henry Fanshawe School, Dronfield

A Sonnet For An Island

Rule Britannia, the words are quoted,
When people comment about our nation,
Pride, wealth and victory are denoted,
Even though we sat in isolation,
That is not to say we were not threatened,
By powerful enemies from afar,
But our strong spirit has never lessened,
We have always been a bright, burning star,
We have never given into evil,
Through the Longest Day, and all the hardship,
We have loved through all the great upheaval
Not to say we've done it without a trip.
But I can say the world won't be ridden,
Of this entity we call Great Britain.

Haydn Walters [12]
Dronfield Henry Fanshawe School, Dronfield

Summer Holidays

You bring fun to everyone including me
You make us all laugh together
And bring us together in one big crowd

Then we leave to go on holiday
Then everyone is driving off shouting hooray
Arriving in the holiday bay
The fun and relaxation takes place

Thousands of families all visiting one area
Where camp sites are full of caravans
With cars full of bags.

Jack Wild [12]
Dronfield Henry Fanshawe School, Dronfield

Ming Ming

This may not rhyme or go in time,
But this isn't about rhyming,
It's about Ming Ming's timing,
Ming Ming is my cat, who likes to sit on mats.

Ming Ming likes to wake me up at six every morning,
This can get very boring;
Fussing her every morning,
This can also be very annoying.

Ming Ming is very friendly,
But she gets very jealous,
When I'm fussing the laptop instead of her,
She gets my attention by head-butting me.

I get lots of dead mice,
It isn't very nice;
When I get half eaten ones in my bed,
Or lying on my head!

That poor little shrew,
Who was in my shoe;
Shaking because of the cat,
Who was sat on the big brown mat.

It's about Ming Ming my cat,
Who likes to sit on mats,
Morning and evening,
She purrs sitting on her mat.

Hannah Murgatroyd (12)
Dronfield Henry Fanshawe School, Dronfield

The Laptop

The lights come on with just a tiny flick,
I open my browser, only one click.
My eyes turn to saucers watching the screen,
This is by far the best thing I've ever seen.
I watch videos while stuck to the chair,
If I'm told to come off now, it's not fair.
Hearing the music my head's up and down,
With my best songs I never have a frown.
I play games all night, the fun never ends,
Go in a chat room and talk to my friends,
The harsh rules to this I sometimes bend.
I detest Twitter, the thought drives me mad,
If MySpace shut down now, I would be glad.
If it goes missing, it feels like lashes,
I like it until the day it crashes.
I want to have the best of its own kind,
All of the best ones I have to find.
I search for every one of the high and low,
And then my Internet breaks and goes slow.
I keep it with me even if it's lead,
I'd take it with me upstairs in my bed,
The love for the laptop will not be dead.

James Sanderson (12)
Dronfield Henry Fanshawe School, Dronfield

Emotions

Love is an excited emotion like hate
The less that I get, the more that I give.
Passion is another emotion I hate
I need it to thrive and live every day.
Intelligence is not an emotion
It's used in many a way to know things.
Strife is like conflict with more devotion
It's used by people whose bells often ring.
But all these emotions have their own way
It's not that they're really very horrid,
They do live with you every night and day
Impossible to erase and get rid,
Emotions aren't bad is what I'm saying,
They are not worth going, they're worth staying.

Callum Hyslop (12)
Dronfield Henry Fanshawe School, Dronfield

The Bennster

Mr Ben, so tiny and small he sleeps a lot curled up in a ball.
He purrs, purrs and sometimes it's loud
He usually does this when he's feeling proud.
His whiskers are long and his tail is too,
He's shiny and black and very affectionate to you!
His emerald eyes that light up so bright
To help him get home in the dead of the night,
His nickname is the 'Bennster'!
But now he is very old
I'll love him forever
Now the story is told.

Rose Burrows (12)
Dronfield Henry Fanshawe School, Dronfield

Football Hell

Man United I'm so excited they're gonna have a match
I need to go catch the bus.
I sit down with a frown,
Man United score, I can't believe what I saw.
There's a crackle in my ears, the crown goes wild,
The match breaks out and there's a massive pile,
Football boots flying, people crying.
There's a big crash as the stadium starts to fall down,
There's no more frown no more,
Please God save me now,
Smash! A helicopter comes
I eat my chocolate buns
I run down.
I grab hold and start to fly away,
The stadium starts to set on fire and we go higher,
Now I know God has faith and I am safe.

Scott Sigsworth (11)
Dronfield Henry Fanshawe School, Dronfield

The Park Fright

The thing that matters to me is the park
I walked to the park last night
I nearly had a fight
And I got quite a big fright
There was a dog running towards me
It jumped on me
And then got off to have a pee
And then it ran away from me.
But now I don't think the park
Really does matter to me.

Adam Burniston (12)
Dronfield Henry Fanshawe School, Dronfield

Sisters Are Keepers

We have our arguments,
make each other cry,
but sisters are keepers until we die.
Bruises and cuts made from anger,
always end up in a bundle of laughter.

My sister is so special to me,
but she doesn't know it.
Me and her are so alike,
in looks and personality.

Me and my sister are like the sun,
we sometimes have a cloudy day,
but the sun still shines on anyway.

Same blood running through our flesh,
makes it harder to forget,
that we are sisters forever and this won't change.

So we will make the most of our childhood,
loving, sharing and having fun.
Make every moment of our lives,
worth living together.

My sister matters to me,
and no one will take away our special relationship.
On and off, hot and cold
you are my sister and I cannot change this
so I will love you till the end.

Madeleine Welch (12)
Dronfield Henry Fanshawe School, Dronfield

My Best Friend

What matters to me,
Is what matters to you,
Because you're my best friend,
Until the very end.

I know you'll be there for me,
Whatever the weather,
Through the pouring rain,
Or the bright sunshine.

Because my friends are like stars,
They come and go,
But the ones that stay,
Are the ones that glow.

If it wasn't for you,
I know I couldn't pull through,
When the times are hard,
You give me the friendship card.

We'll be best friends forever,
We'll stand by each other,
Because when one of us falls,
We fall together.

But as well as our downs,
We have our ups,
And - when we laugh,
I think we laugh too much.

So just remember,
What matters to me,
Is what matters to you,
And three more words . . . I love you.

Lucy Rose (12)
Dronfield Henry Fanshawe School, Dronfield

My Poem On Golf

If I had to choose one most important thing
Golf would come first by far
Golf takes away the stress from school
As I finish the first hole with a par.

It gives me a sense of achievement
And something I strive towards
I've made new friends and relationships
And also won many awards.

When I play for my county (Derbyshire)
I feel so excited and proud
But when I approach the first tee
I feel nervous in front of the crowd.

When I play as part of a team
I feel full of passion and pride
I know I can win and do my best
With the confidence I feel inside!

James Wadsworth (13)
Dronfield Henry Fanshawe School, Dronfield

School

School, school, everyone says it's not cool,
I never really liked primary school.
Neither did anyone else
I liked it when I was younger,
even though, I was naughtier.
As soon as I heard ding dong from the bell
in a dash, I was out of school
but I fell in a well!
That's exactly when I had a big thought
that I knew, I never liked school,
and thought it was so uncool.

Katie Ruddiforth (11)
Dronfield Henry Fanshawe School, Dronfield

Christmas

Christmas is here, I hope it will snow,
Santa is coming - down my chimney, 'Ho, ho!'
Presents and chocolate, what a wonderful day,
I'll eat it all - let my teeth decay.

I run downstairs hoping for the best,
I look out the window, the snow is there!
I wake up my sister by tugging her hair,
Bang goes the present as I drop it on the floor,
This Christmas is great I want more!

Dinner next - the presents have gone,
I get chocolate and a toffee bonbon,
What a great Christmas!

Liam Skinner (11)
Dronfield Henry Fanshawe School, Dronfield

What I Like

My hobbies
I love to dive but I don't make much splash
but it's over in a flash.
I play football and get covered in mud
and fall over in the mud
I bmx but when I fall
I curl up in a ball

My pets
I have a cat but it
always brings home rats.
I love cats, dogs, pigs and frogs.
We have a dog and it gets
covered in mud and we clean him all up.

Elliot Beeden (12)
Dronfield Henry Fanshawe School, Dronfield

Friends

Starting school is always cruel,
But my friends are great,
My friends are cool,
Here's a poem for them.

When I started St Andrew's,
Me and Henry weren't good friends,
But once we settled in,
We let our friendship begin.

Charlotte B and Chloe,
At Fanshawe we met,
But once we were talking,
Good friends we started to get.

James and Liam,
I already knew,
But little did I know,
I'd be in the same form as you.

Steph, Lucy and Charlotte T,
At St Andrew's they were,
And once again,
I'm in a class with her, her and her.

In a class with Connor,
A great fashion designer,
Steph and Cuff going out,
She'll be his first buyer.

Thomas Asquith (11)
Dronfield Henry Fanshawe School, Dronfield

My Family

My mum and dad,
My mum and dad,
Went on their very first date
They sat at a restaurant talking as they ate

My family,
My family,
Started with a ping,
Ever since my mum got her wedding ring

I was here,
I was here,
What a happy day
In a small, cramped incubator I lay

My sister came,
My sister came,
With a little bang,
My dad rang his mum, excited as he rang

It's been exciting,
It's been exciting,
The years have gone in a flash
I'm growing up oh no!
My moods are going to clash.

Lucy Mae Baker (12)
Dronfield Henry Fanshawe School, Dronfield

Dancing

What matters to me is always dancing
Saturday morning my dad calls it prancing
My nan and her friends, they run it like mad
Not everyone turns up, it's stressful and sad
St Andrew's is where we go
They don't let us stand on our toes
Otherwise we'll break them and shake them
Until we can wake them
From this dreadful dream
That I cannot see

From Grade 1 to Grade 2 to Grade 3 to Grade 4
Sometimes it gets boring and you're wishing for no more
You talk to your friends and then get told off
Please oh please why can't it stop?
But I'm just joking
Soon I will be poking
Where everyone knows
The shoes where you stand on your toes.

Stephanie Ashmore (11)
Dronfield Henry Fanshawe School, Dronfield

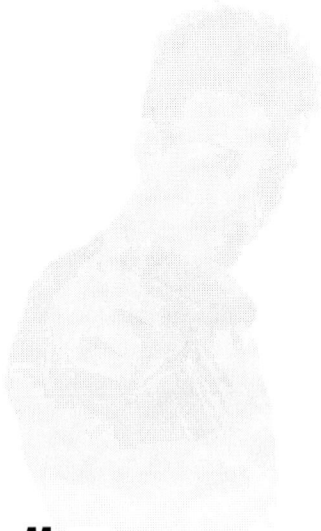

My Train

The train that I want will be
speedy not slow
The train that I get will be faster
than a tornado
Only the best of coals will make my
train steam
Whilst you stand at the station and
watch the paint gleam

Now take off the brakes and let
the train go
Let's make it go speedy don't make
it go slow
C'mon through the country let's whistle
at the sheep
The cars will be so proud they're
bound to beep!

Connor Hulatt (11)
Dronfield Henry Fanshawe School, Dronfield

Gymnastics

I twist and turn way up high,
I tumble and leap in the sky,

As I cartwheel everywhere,
Up the stairs or anywhere,

I do loads of splits and spins
If I do it right I get grins,

I do loads and loads of training
Even when it is raining,

Even when I do it wrong
I get back up and try to be strong.

But . . .
I love gymnastics
I love what I do.

Charlotte Matthews (11)
Dronfield Henry Fanshawe School, Dronfield

World Of Pets

Dogs and cats are really cool,
even if most of them drool,
they're crazy, quirky and really kind,
even if they annoy you a lot of the time
you just don't mind!

Fish and parrots crazy as they are,
great pets, great mates,
no one, nothin' can stop you lovin' them.

Rabbits are bouncy and bonny,
sometimes called a bunny,
they're funny,
they're cuddly.

When they are outside they are lively,

Gerbils, well how cute are they,
they have chubby little cheeks,
to eat all of the hay,
big round eyes,
and don't forget they are fluffy like cotton.

So in conclusion pets
should rule the world.

Lauren Kaye (12)
Dronfield Henry Fanshawe School, Dronfield

Friendship!

My best friend for life,
Someone who's caring and nice,
Someone who makes me laugh,
Who helps me, say in maths.

Someone who I can share secrets with,
Someone who can have a good time and live.

A friend who you can turn to when you're sad,
A friend who calms you down when you're mad!

A friendship that can always mend,
My best friend!

Charlotte Taylor (11)
Dronfield Henry Fanshawe School, Dronfield

My Dog, My Dog!

My dog, my dog, I love my dog
My dog he likes to say woof
My dog, my dog, I love my dog
He's small so he isn't very tough.

Football, football, my favourite sport
Even though I'm quite short
I play on the fields every Sunday
The season finishes in May.

James Lawson (11)
Dronfield Henry Fanshawe School, Dronfield

Fashion, Stars And Passion

My passion,
for my fashion.
Models, stars,
Clubs and bars.
My passion,
for my fashion.

Cats, dogs,
Pigs and frogs.
My passion,
for my fashion.
New Look, Primark,
Topshop, Lipsy.

Charlotte Louise Banfield (11)
Dronfield Henry Fanshawe School, Dronfield

Animals

Animals, animals,
I love animals,
My favourite animal is a
White tiger!

Animals, animals,
I love animals,
I love all the animals
In the world!

Chloe Leigh Hale (12)
Dronfield Henry Fanshawe School, Dronfield

Seaside

We like the sea
So does Ann-Marie,
Fishes swimming under the sea,
I like the sea.

We like the sun,
So we'll all have fun,
Perhaps a sandy bun,
I like the sun.

We like the sand,
Getting tanned,
With the beach manned,
I like the sand.

We like the rock pools,
Riding on the mules,
Crabs jumping into be cool,
I like the rock pool.

Alice Wood (11)
Dronfield Henry Fanshawe School, Dronfield

Water Fight

Every year in the summer holidays,
we go out on the avenue,
to call for friends,
to come out and play.
we gather all the equipment
out and set.

The next minute,
water balloons, water guns and mega shooters,
shoot all over the road,
wetting people,
from head to toes.
splish, splosh, splash, drip, drop, plop.

Eventually at the end, we all fade away,
we all fade away,
pack away, ready for next year.
only one person will be left standing,
holding the water trophy.

Daniel Barden (11)
Dronfield Henry Fanshawe School, Dronfield

Untitled

Strangely I like cricket
But I never hit the wicket.
My sporting skills are great,
And I play it with my mate.
I can slog the ball 200 yards,
With my favourite golf club

I am a menace at tennis,
Yet I'd rather climb a crevice.
Sometimes I do like swimming,
In tests I'd rather be winning.
In fields I enjoy throwing
In the garden I like mowing.

Fraser Nunns (11)
Dronfield Henry Fanshawe School, Dronfield

Books

I love to read books
maybe about my good looks
maybe an adventure one
or the one about the giant's big tongue
I can't put books down
but if I don't have one I'm sure to frown

Although books are not my life
they're better than cutting food with a knife
I love to read in the sunshine and the dark
I must have over a million bookmarks
I love to read splash and bang
but I have nightmares about giant fangs.

Andrew Lunn (11)
Dronfield Henry Fanshawe School, Dronfield

Mr A

(To Mr Anderson my old head teacher who will never be forgotten!)

Mr A I'd like to say that you're a great man,
Every day used to think or say that I'm a big fan,
When you said goodbye just now,
A goodbye, a sigh, you were off, *kapow!*
But wait, you left your corn beef hash!
Crawling down through everyone's toes,
Sniffing it out with his great nose.

You were always loaded on the dinner,
Always polite as he wasn't a sinner.
So we don't want him to go now, even the cat wouldn't miaow.
If he threw a disco in San Francisco
The entire city would join the calypso.
So when he goes back to the home and the hob,
One thing's for sure everyone will sob!

Mr A you're really cool,
Always funny and acting the fool.
I remember when you dressed up in a wig!
Acting all daft,
Just like a kid.

When Mr A disappeared,
Every living thing burst into tears.

Beck Shillito (11)
Dronfield Henry Fanshawe School, Dronfield

Cake

When the smell of fresh cake drifts round the house,
It drags everyone to the kitchen.
They all ask for a bowl full,
But only get half.

There's like a crunchy crust on the top,
Then the crunching in your mouth.
Everyone eats it hot,
Then pay for it by the pain of indigestion.

Everyone swallowing,
And the sound of gulping around the room.
Then everyone says, 'Mmmm that was nice'
And Mum gets all the credit.

Charlie Hollingworth (11)
Dronfield Henry Fanshawe School, Dronfield

The T-Rex Bellyache

The T-rex has a bellyache,
You better stay out of his way
If you ever get lost,
Just hide up a tree all day.

Listen for a crash!
Look out for smash!
You may want to make a quick grave,
And bury all your cash.

If you hear a roar!
Just take a quick glance,
At that moment you might just want to,
Change your pants!

James Harrison (12)
Dronfield Henry Fanshawe School, Dronfield

What Matters

What matters to me?
What matters to you?
It could be a book,
It could be a shoe!
What matters to me is . . .
My family! Of course,
My friends too,
They are my special things,
I shall treasure them forever,
Let them go? Never!
Splash! Oops that's me and my friends,
The fun, it never ends!
Smash! Ha, that's my big brother,
I know who will have something to say,
My mother!
What matters to me?
What matters to you?
It could be a book,
It could be a shoe!
What matters to me are . . .
Animals!
Buzz, buzz, buzz go the bees
Clip, clip, clop goes the horse
Woof, woof, howl goes the dog
What matters to me? What matters to you?
A lot matters to me,

What about you?

Sophie Louise Hamilton (11)
Dronfield Henry Fanshawe School, Dronfield

Rabbits

Rabbits are cute
Rabbits are wonderful
Rabbits run in the long grass.
Rabbits munch on carrots;
When you and I are together you know I love you.
How you run so fast as fast as the wind,
How you sense danger from a couple of feet away.
How you stamp your feet if you've found something,
How you sniff with your nose to smell a different scent.
How you use your ears to hear something;
How you use your paws to dig underground.
How you whizz past other rabbits.
How you use your claws to scratch another rabbit
to do as he is told.
How your eyes are like a shimmering moon,
How your whiskers tickle my face.
How your tail is soft as soft as my pillow
How your fur is so soft that I want to hug you.
That is why I love rabbits.

Paris Rose Wykes (11)
Dronfield Henry Fanshawe School, Dronfield

Animals

I like going horse riding hearing the sound of its hooves
clashing against the road,
clip-clop, clip-clop over and over again,
until you get to the field galloping through the corn.
The corn makes a swish noise as I go on riding
through the flattened corn.

Dolphins, splashing through the water
pounding into the massive waves and then . . .
comes the orca the biggest family member of the dolphin,
the pod dominates the whole of the ocean
the water pounds against the rocks
making a crashing, smashing sound.

Dogs, wagging their tail and panting after a long walk
at the dog park.
Barking at each other as they play
so they all go home and slurp down their ice-cold water
and have a nap.

Isabelle Davies (11)
Dronfield Henry Fanshawe School, Dronfield

The Fox . . .

Quickly it ran through the forest,
its white-tipped tail above the grass,
it really was very fast.

The snuffling of its black nose,
where is it coming from?
Nobody knows.

Black and white ears and shiny brown eyes,
shifting across the land,
extremely sly.

Red fur through red poppies,
padded feet across squelchy marsh,
bumbling bees and creepy-crawlies . . .

. . . then . . .

. . . it pounced on a bird from the bird box;
it was . . . a fox.

April Bentley (11)
Dronfield Henry Fanshawe School, Dronfield

Animals

Elephants are big,
and go splash in puddles.
They are crinkly and grey,
but never disobey.

Pandas are cuddly,
and go croak as they move.
They are large and sleepy,
but not at all creepy.

Giraffe's are tall,
and chomp all day long.
They are colourful and bright,
and also very nice.

These animals matter to me,
because they are all very friendly.
So I hope they matter to you too,
and that you appreciate them as much as I do!

Laura Critchley (11)
Dronfield Henry Fanshawe School, Dronfield

Football!

Roar! went the crowd and the teams were shivering,
The ref stood, whistle in his mouth,
The toot toot of the whistle led the game,
The ball flew as it did last match, it was exactly the same
The ball came to me, goal in sight, I had a go, the ball curved in flight,
'A post? How?' I cried,
I told the ref it was a goal but he knew I lied,
I looked back and chased the ball
Tackled again so I pretended to fall
'Ow, ow!' I screamed, but
I got a yellow for faking.
The opposition had a shot.
Closer it came,
Closer . . .
Bam! Right in the face!
'Timothy!' screamed the teacher.
'Stop dreaming and get on with your test.
And stop pretending your rubber is a football!'

Mohammed Ghani (11)
Dronfield Henry Fanshawe School, Dronfield

My Dog

My dog is cool, his name is Tazz,
He fell in the pool and had a bit of a frazz,
Tazz has a friend, her name is Molly,
She is a bit big, happy and jolly,
Also there's Tia, who likes to jump off the pier,
With a smash and a howl she hits the water,
Molly thinks that Tia's her daughter,
With a big growl she sets off into the water,
But Tia comes back, and Molly looks like a soaking Big Mac,
Whilst Tazz just sits and laughs,
Molly and Tia both have baths,
Tazz is nearly five years old,
When he sits on you it's never cold!
Tazz likes chips; he fights with the cat,
He's had a few clips, and wet bits where cats have spat,
He gets a bit slippy, but he isn't that fat,
He gets very trippy, his hair goes mad!
He falls off the sofa but never gets sad,
When he eats peppers he goes really mad,
My dog is amazing his name is Tazz.

Joe Leverton (11)
Dronfield Henry Fanshawe School, Dronfield

Ice Hockey Poem

Team comes on with thundering cheer
Music playing in the background
All the lights flicker on as Steeler Dan appears
The game starts, an old man farts
As the puck is slashed, crashing into the wall
Penalty is shouted
As he is clouted, there's blood everywhere
There's a crack in the ice
It isn't very nice because the blood is still there
The ice is fixed, the players get mixed,
Smack! Goes the puck into the back of the goal
The goalie falls over and gets his bum wet
And when all said and done
It goes to prove that Steelers are number 1!

Bethany Jayne Scivill (12)
Dronfield Henry Fanshawe School, Dronfield

My Dog

Joe is cute
and cool, he
has always been
a fool.
Sometimes bites
but that's alright.
He's nine months old,
he's nearly getting old.
He's always sad but I make him glad.
He is always falling in the pond.
Splash! And if I take him for a walk,
he would splash in the puddles and
every time we want to fetch a ball,
it would always land on the window sill.

Jordan Roddis (11)
Dronfield Henry Fanshawe School, Dronfield

Dancing Exam

The music starts!
I do a jump and a twirl,
I do a split jump in the air,
A buzzing fly comes in as I do the splits.
It annoys me as I come back up,
As I do a back bend in a flump.
As the music went ping I did a pose,
My heart started racing,
It was the end!
The croaky voice of the woman said, 'Goodbye!'
I took a curtsey,
I was finished,
I ran to the door.
I was so glad to be off the horrible dance floor!

Abigail Wright (11)
Dronfield Henry Fanshawe School, Dronfield

My Dog

I love my dog,
he is so big,
he is so hairy
so that makes him look scary.
He goes running through
the puddles going splash,
splash, splash.
Woof, woof, woof
as he barks at the neighbours
water dripping from his black fur.
He has sharp black claws.
and that's about my dog.

Danielle Garton (11)
Dronfield Henry Fanshawe School, Dronfield

Family

To have a family with you is like being at school,
Like having a big group of friends round you every day,
Each of them different in their own special way,
They will help when somehow you act like a fool.

Parents can help when you need reassuring,
Brothers and sisters will help when something is boring.
Animals can also be part of your family,
But no matter what you will always live happily.

Emily Skinner [11]
Eastwood Comprehensive School, Nottingham

My Family

When I'm not with you I feel like dying and crying,
Though when I'm with you
I feel like I have something to live for.
Then I'm smiling, because I feel like flying.

Sometimes we act like a mad house.
When something is upsetting we're there for each other.

We fight and squabble and even cry.
But we all know that it's going to blow over.
Because we all try.

Being a family is the best thing ever.
If it wasn't for them,
I wouldn't have a life like this to treasure!

Chloe Benniston [12]
Eastwood Comprehensive School, Nottingham

My Mum

She is my best friend,
A friend who is always there,
She loves and cares for me,
And hugs me when I'm scared.

She finds a way to make me smile,
And when I smile it goes a 100 miles,
If it wasn't for my mum,
I wouldn't be here today,
So now I would just like to say,
I love you so much
And I love you more and more
Every single day!

Lucy Brown (12)
Eastwood Comprehensive School, Nottingham

A Friend

A friend is like a shade tree beside a summer way,
A friend is like the sunshine that makes a perfect day,
A friend is like a flower that's worn close to the heart,
A friend is like a treasure with which one will not part.
A friend makes you happy even when you're down,
A friend is always a jewel
So precious as can be.

Nicole McPhilbin (12)
Eastwood Comprehensive School, Nottingham

Freedom For Whales

Whales and dolphins should be free.
Porpoises should swim happily.
As it is, dolphins must stay
In tiny pools, locked away.
No fish, no fun, no friends at all,
Diving through hoops with the same old ball.
Whales are hunted for their meat.
For cretaceans, life just isn't sweet.
It's just not fair, as they're sweet and kind,
But in marine parks, humans think they don't mind
Being in a chlorinated tank,
With rubbish and dung making the water rank.
They have feelings, like us, too.
What they need is people like you,
Who care for sealife quite a lot,
And think whalers have lost the plot.
Give money to the WDCS,
Save dolphins from pools, whaling ships and fishing nets.
Whales and dolphins should be free.
Porpoises should swim happily.

Molly Alexandra Heafford (11)
Hollygirt School, Nottingham

What Matters . . . Through My Eyes

Four walls surrounding, white as snow.
Rain ticking in the background, singing the songs of perished.
Come back to me again the shepherd of the damned.
Light has become an enemy,
And darkness my closest friend.
Lustre fades away never to adorn my face again.
Surely, as we lie among the deceased.

Days to go on like eternity.
But I am still standing by your side.
We can chase away this veiledness
Hand inside hand - I'll hold you tight.
If you fall then so will I.

Leaves fall to black,
As the skies return to grey.
Hope fills the heart,
And breaks away.
Cold air above us,
White blacks out again.

There is nothing left of you!
It's written all in your eyes,
Holding onto your breath?
Why do you care?
Breathe your last breath, and say the last goodbye.

I keep holding, crying for you, but I can't bring you back to life.
Say goodbye to the Devil . . . and welcome this new life.

Aisha Tanveer (15)
Hollygirt School, Nottingham

My Family

My family have fallouts.
My mum and dad are divorced.
My mum and sister don't get on.
My dad found a new lady.
My mum has found a new man.
Me, I just get stuck in the middle of it.

But my mum, my dad,
My sister all love me and
That's all that matters to me.

Rebecca Collingham (11)
Hollygirt School, Nottingham

Poem Writing

I am writing a poem
I'm not as good as them
I try to rhyme
I don't get paid for it, if I did it would be a dime
Poetry is not what I do
When it comes to poetry, I haven't got a clue
How do you get famous from writing a few lines?
It's annoying and should be a crime.

If you want a proper story
Something rude and gory
I know what to do
I'm probably better than you
I'll make you read for ages
I'll make you go through emotional stages
Making millions from my books
While people in the room give me looks
I'll be the one laughing in five years' time.

Stephanie Muir
Hollygirt School, Nottingham

Summer Sounds

S ounds of nature all around,
U p in the trees are the birds tweeting a sound,
M assive trees towering down - keep us cool all day,
M agic green spiky grass where children play,
E veryone happy to play all night,
R unning around the park holding a kite.

D ancing around doing everything you want to do,
A ll people trying not to step in bird poo!
Y ellow sun beaming down,
S ounds of nature all around!

Zoe Woodiwiss (12)
Hollygirt School, Nottingham

Wild Tiger

Tigers are wild
Tigers have claws and fangs.
They live in wild jungles
Some of them at the zoo.

They hunt for their prey
They eat and sleep every day.
As they rip their prey with their scary claws
And sharp fangs.

Tigers are as dangerous as lions
Their environment is savage
And feral as they are.

Arwa Elemam (12)
Manning School for Girls, Aspley

As A Child

As a child,
I saw the beauty in everything.
No maths or science clouded my path.
The meaning of life was 'just because it can'
And I saw the world through tinted glasses,
There was no wrong.

My parents knew,
Knew the day would come when I would no longer see
The universe as my playground
And the reality I lived in malleable.
So they left me ignorant, in the dark, in my eyes, the light,
To protect me from life's hardships.

When I look back,
On my salad days, I realise that life is no better now,
Than when I was a child, in fact it is worse.
But that was to come.
If I had been as naïve all my life,
Would I be as I am today?

I see now,
That in my youth, I was secluded, but at the same time free,
Until the day more came to stay, to live,
Teased me, jeered me, my life was inverted,
When I was alone I was surrounded,
When I was surrounded I was alone.

I took salvation,
In a thing which saved me, made me who I am,
Decrypting this reality, knowing how it worked,
Math and science opened my eyes and my mind,
But at the cost of shutting out my heart,
And all desires of the flesh.

Then I grew stoic,
Only feeling towards things I had contributed to or made,
This caused me to consider military life, and, going through with it,
I barely smiled as I learned new tactics,
Felt fulfilled that I could tell myself a had discipline,
But never truly consummated.

But one evening,
As I once again experimented, trying to find meaning in my life,
I slipped unconscious in an accident,
In which my mind was torn asunder,
Where I realised that I had to find the balance between
Glacial and warm-hearted.

I am still on that quest,
I doubt it will ever truly be resolved, but for now,
I have learned to take a joke, even told a few,
And can feel very deeply if need be,
But that cold, controlled air that stays about me
Will be there until eternity's end.

Yasmin Alexander (13)
Manning School for Girls, Aspley

A Squatter's Life For Me

To be homeless and nomadic
Is to be without ownership of houses made of brick.
It is to be under the stars,
Resting in abandoned, broken down cars.

Hiking from place to place,
Meeting many a new face.
Scrounging food, money and clothes
Following which ever way the wind blows.

Since the government shut me down,
I've been walking from town to town.
Not one soul allowing me accommodation,
All because I lost my occupation.

No settled plot to call my own,
I've become so very alone,
All I want is a familiar place,
An 'owned by me' space.

But alas, my home changes time after time,
Becoming any place I can find.
From barn to shack to tree
This is a squatters life for me . . .

Maya Johnston (14)
Manning School for Girls, Aspley

The Dancer Of Her Mind

She watches the dancers perform, on TV and live,
The wistfulness and longing cutting her like a knife.
She longs to be able to move like them, graceful and free:
But it isn't meant to be.
She is a prisoner, trapped in her body.
Her body is weak: it limits her in many ways:
She is forced to stand and gaze
At the people twirling, whirling: doing what she yearns to do.

She tries to dance, tries and tries.
She pushes her body over the limit, she pushes until tears come to her eyes.
She pushes too far and collapses to the ground with a melancholy wail.
She gets up and tries again, but all to no avail.
Her body screams at her, telling her to stop and give up her dancing dream.
But she doesn't want to and pushes her body to the extreme.
She knows her dream is blind
Her body just isn't designed,

To be like the dancer of her mind.

Paige Walker (13)
Manning School for Girls, Aspley

Goose Fair

Dazzling lights makes wonderful
Horrifying ghost trains nervous
Mouth-watering food makes me ravenous
Fast rides make me dizzy.
Ghost walks make me scared
And I get lost and I can't find my way around
Sticky sweets give me a toothache
Bumpy rides make me sick
Spinning rides makes me scared
Twister rides give me stomache.

Samina Mohammed [11]
Manning School for Girls, Aspley

The Fair

The fair was cold when I went on the ghost train.
The fizzing cold drink tickled my tongue.
The noisy people made me feel frightened.
The yummy hot dogs were delicious.
The music was fantastic
When I went home I was tired but I had fun.
The colourful lights blinded me.
Me and my friends went on a massive ride
It was fast as a racing car.
The toddlers laughing happily made me smile.

Claire Atkinson [11]
Manning School for Girls, Aspley

Goose Fair

Bright lights flashing in my eyes making me feel blinded,
Rapid rides made me feel sick,
The cold drinks tickled my tongue,
Fresh fudge made me feel peckish,
Noisy people gave me a headache,
Mouth-watering food all around me.

The scary ghost train made me feel startled,
Gigantic rides made me feel nervous,
Fabulous atmosphere makes me feel squashed,
Ear-splitting music gives me a dancing mood,
Chatty children were making me feel bored,
Ear popping screaming hurt my ears.

On the way out I walked past a speaker, it nearly deafened me.
I felt really tired and it was very dark
And on the way home I went to KFC.

When I went to Goose Fair I felt really blissful and jolly,
And the crowd made us feel stressed.

Lauren Hall (12)
Manning School for Girls, Aspley

Autumn Is Back

Autumn is back.
Dark brings loneliness.
Leaves are getting close to death,

What will autumn bring for us?

Leaves are flying everywhere.
Weather has changed,
Windy, snowy and rainy.
Brown leaves on the ground.

Quiet all around
Now is the end of a tree's life!

Areeba Umar (13)
Manning School for Girls, Aspley

Cheetah

She grips the throne with claws of steel.
Quickly she glances at her midday meal.
Pouncing proudly she catches her prey.
She quickly knows that today is her day.

Finishing her dinner.
She turns to a pond.
Dips her head down and becomes quite fond,
Of the refreshing cooling liquid.
As still as a statue she becomes again,
Drifting off into her dream.

Morgan Marriott (11)
Manning School for Girls, Aspley

Midnight Wolf

Trees reach so high,
A moonlight so bright in the lonely sky.
And then a wolf striding along,
With eyes as silver as steel,
Sparkling stars like glowing gems in the midnight sky.

His sharp, shocking teeth so jagged,
Looking for prey,
Under the mist on the ground,
Low spirits crying for help.
Damp and quiet.
Gloomy and shadowy.
Then a wild rabbit scurries along,
And then the wolf leaps up like a piranha fish,
And catches the wild rabbit,
With his monsterous claws,
And down the rabbit goes,
His souls reaches the tangly trees within,
Up, up, up the ghost goes and then he turns into a
Shooting star.

Sara Abbas (12)
Manning School for Girls, Aspley

The Dog

He sprinted towards the dirty stick,
He licked and licked with some joy,
Then he twirled in the green grass,

After a while he stood and smiled,
Then the daft dog laughed,
Just like a howling hyena.

Laila Ahmed (11)
Manning School for Girls, Aspley

The Tiger

As you look his beady eyes stare,
Straight into you.
And like the wind, he moves rapidly.
As he runs, his tail balances.
The wind in the jungle howls.
He runs in the leafy, emerald nature.
Ripping his delicious prey, safe from others.

Alisha Hussain (11)
Manning School for Girls, Aspley

The Cat

He's sleeping in the land of nod
Sleeping peacefully
Purring whilst being stroked

Slowly awakening with alert eyes
He blends in the trees, watching his prey
And like a tiger he pursues his dinner.

Erin Attaway (12)
Manning School for Girls, Aspley

The Dog

As she bolted toward the blue flowers, she bit a buzzy bee,
Close to leaves falling from a tree,
Sat in the garden she itches because of a flea.

The almost micro bugs scatter inbetween the grass,
She peers from above perched on a path,
And like an interested scientist, she howls at the grass.

Ruby Galway (11)
Manning School for Girls, Aspley

Mystery!

He strolls in the midnight jungle,
Waiting for his prey,
His eyes are silver, steel, just as the moonlight shines.
The sunshine has come,
The birds are singing,
While the big, scary beast strikes again

He's loud with sharp piranha jaws and marmalade skin,
What's furry, spotty and smells like gin?
He shoots like a shooting rocket,
Until he's back under the midnight moon.

Veera Kaur (11)
Manning School for Girls, Aspley

The Snow Tiger

Its beautiful fur shines in the snow,
As it strolls it glows and glows.

As it leaps from stone to stone,
There it roars, his big mouth moans.

The tiger's prey moves very slow,
The tiger will catch it, look at it go.

As the tiger lies around,
The pure white snow falls on the ground.

Emily Holloway (11) & Mimi Tien (12)
Manning School for Girls, Aspley

The Lion Poem

When he runs, he's as fast as a cheetah.
As he runs, the wind strokes his bushy mane.
But as he stands still, he is as still as a statue.
His mane blows wearily in the light breeze, softly against his beady eyes.

The atmosphere is humid as the sun.
Vines and leaves from trees flutter down like butterflies.
Around the corner a sneaky hyena waits for you!

Safiyah Sohail (11)
Manning School for Girls, Aspley

Free

She stood there,
With that graceful beauty,
So breathtaking, it's as if she fell from the majestic heaven itself,
Skipping with such elegance.
You couldn't spot a fault anywhere.

But then humungous hands came hurrying through the bristly brambles.
She fled, running and running.
Until she fell silently going up to the place she really belonged to.
Now she was truly free.

Sofia India Starz Falade (12)
Manning School for Girls, Aspley

The Furry Kitten Symber

The furry body as soft as pure feather,
Sneaking as quiet as a small spider creeping.

Eyes as beautiful as the blanket blue ocean waves.
Quiet as a snail slithering across the garden.

A happy house full of loving owners and chatty friends.
She glances with her delicate bright eyes.
Looking out carefully for any danger or prey.

Sabah Iqbal (12)
Manning School for Girls, Aspley

My Fluffy Friend

She pounced on the soft ground
Observing the big city around
Having to hear the immense sound

Swishing her tail as she stands
Having white paws like sensitive hands
With the habitat of flourishing lands.

Alina Ali (11)
Manning School for Girls, Aspley

The Mouse

The trembling, tense little mouse,
Watching with his beady eyes,
Listening with his leafy ears.
Suddenly pouncing off with fear,
As the big house cat comes near.
The big pieces of furniture blocking his way,
As he's running far away.
He's running like a crazy cheetah.
The cat shows him who's teacher.

Aqsa Abbas (11)
Manning School for Girls, Aspley

The Tiger

The velvet tiger, with crimson eyes
Walks through the jungle with destined paws
As still as a statue he stands.
The jungles, flowers and trees are growing
The lakes and the streams are fastly flowing
In his kingdom he is at the top, soon though he will drop . . .
Lightly
Lost
Forever.

Megan Truswell (11)
Manning School for Girls, Aspley

The Lion

He moves through the jungle so green
Faster than a rocket trying not to be seen
The grass is flaming and the trees are growing
Their eyes meet, both are glowing

The jungle before him is quiet
He still has his prey in his sight
Could it really end right?
Could it be another win to this fight?

Samaira Saleem (11)
Manning School for Girls, Aspley

The Hamster

On the lookout the handsome hairy hamster hides,
He is putrid like a rubbish bin,
On the lookout over his cage,
Wary over his little kingdom.

His clumsy silly movements,
In the sawdust he stumbles,
He saunters over to his wheel,
The noise is like an electric drill.

Heidi Hylands-Vizzard (12)
Manning School for Girls, Aspley

The Lion

With great force he stamps his furry paw,
In the damp, dark jungle he leaves his trail,
He glances above into the indigo sky.

The crinkled leaves beneath him wrinkle,
As he is paralysed to the spot staring at his prey,
And like a comet shooting to Earth,
He catches his hopeless little prey.

Shanza Akhtar (11)
Manning School for Girls, Aspley

It's All About Me!

S miley Shannon smiling away,
H aving a great time of her life.
A lways got that cheeky grin on her face.
N ever ever frowns.
N either on miserable days.
O bedient on days of days.
N oisy days make her raise.

R ainy days still never wash that grin off her face.
O n the roll, brightens up the teacher's day.
T oday of days brings gifts to her life.
H aving the great days of her lifetime.

Shannon Roth (11)
Manning School for Girls, Aspley

My Lucky

L ovely little bunny
U nhappy sometimes
C ute as ever
K icking every time
Y ou are so lovely.

Haseeba Raja (11)
Manning School for Girls, Aspley

The Autumn Poem

It's cold now and the leaves are beginning to fall.
All they do is cry,
I think I'm motionless.
I don't cry or sob or weep.

I've seen the first leaf fall again
Just hoping, praying that's my baby niece.

I've seen the sunshine turn to rain
And happiness just disappear.

As the stars shine bright at night
All I need to do is look up at the calm night sky.

Like the last leaf on the tree
I know she will come down to me.

Elizabeth Elsom (12)
Manning School for Girls, Aspley

Emotional Poem!

It's dull outside,
And freezing cold.
There's leaves flying around,
And birds hibernating.
The grass cutter's gone and
We're all alone.

Summer has gone and
Autumn has come.
Winter's right next door.

A dead tree with no leaves,
Standing there in front of me.
Why oh why does this happen?

One last leaf on the tree,
Will fall gently in my hand.

Here is autumn,
Right here on the doorstep.

Zara Idrees (12)
Manning School for Girls, Aspley

My Home

My home,
My home is warm and cosy,
Loud and noisy,
Quiet and tense,

I've got two brothers who are like chimpanzees,
They are annoying but I know I can trust them
With anything.

My mum's like a dolphin,
Likes everything quiet and neat,
But she likes to have a joke.

My dad is like a shark,
Likes everything calm,
But when you get on the bad side of him
You will know what time it is.

My house is kind of amazing,
There's always something going on,
It's never quiet, always alive.

But that's what makes my family,
And I love them no matter what!

Demi Waldram (12)
Manning School for Girls, Aspley

Autumn Is Here

The wind is blowing
The leaves are flowing.

All I keep saying is autumn.

Just to hear the first
Crunch of a leaf makes me
Feel overjoyed.

When I see the leaves flowing
Makes me want to flow with them.

Samiya Latif (12)
Manning School for Girls, Aspley

Natural Beauty

Come on, wake up
You don't need that make-up
Natural beauty is the best
It makes you stand out from the rest
You don't need that lippy to go to the chippy.

All you need is a dress
Come on, who are you trying to impress?

So wipe it off with a table cloth
So you don't get more dots
By that I mean your spots!

Shanelle Rowe (12)
Manning School for Girls, Aspley

My Reflection

Look at me,
I'm not what I used to be.
I look at pictures,
That's not me.
I'm sick of people staring at me.

You keep on lying to me,
That's not how I used to be.
I'm still me,
Why can't you just say what you see?

Look at me,
I used to be a lovely young lady.
I'm still me,
Nobody can change me,
Let me be what I want to see.

You keep on lying to me,
Please be honest with me.
People keep on laughing at me.
Why do you keep laughing at me?
Talk to me!

Kimberly Butler (12) & Fatima Angum (12)
Manning School for Girls, Aspley

Brother

Whoever knew that a little man like you
Could be so helpful
When you don't want him to
He makes me laugh when I need to cry
He nicks my lipstick, don't ask why.

He's my friend and my enemy
All wrapped up in one
He's a devil in disguise
He must be the chosen one.

He runs around like a mad little goblin
But if he comes near me
He'll end up hobbling
But no matter what we do
We always say 'I love you.'

Chloe Innes (12)
Manning School for Girls, Aspley

Night Of The Doom Bird

As it swoops through the trees,
Its frightening shadow flies across the gardens,
Only on that certain night,
The doom bird rises.

Lock away your sons and daughters,
Or you'll never see them again,
Lost to its pure black talons,
Only on that certain night,
The doom bird rises.

Hunted by nothing,
Its eyes as black as its soul,
Only on that certain night,
The doom bird rises.

The moon is full,
Shining really bright,
Because today is the 13th,
The bird of death is back,
Only on that certain night,
Well,
Tonight the doom bird rises!

Chelsea Taylor (12)
Manning School for Girls, Aspley

Dreams

Parents sometimes live through their children.
They tell them so much about what they have to be,
That they start to believe it too.

But what about us? What about our dreams?
Dreams shouldn't only be for when you sleep.
They should be achieved,
They should be put from our minds and into action.

We are people
We are privileged
We are ourselves
And we matter.

Clayre Toms (15)
Manning School for Girls, Aspley

The Food Was Mouth-Watering And Delicious

The bungee jumping made me sick
When I went to the big wheel
When I got to the top
I had a beautiful of the fair
The doughnut was fantastic
I loved every minute of it
The baby ride was very slow
And all you can hear was them screaming softly
And the ghost train was so exciting
And the haunted house was freaky.

Tammi Blant (12)
Manning School for Girls, Aspley

All About My Cat Called . . .

All about my cat called . . .
He is tall
He is sharp
He is too cool for school
He is strong long, fun
He is small.

Lucianna Ingram [12]
Manning School for Girls, Aspley

Juwayria

J okey Juwayria
U nlike animals
W ants everything
A nd loves games.
Y ellow's favourite colour
R ates everyone
I nk's horrible
A rt's cool

K asel name
O ctopus are scared
U niversity older
S nakes are horrible
E aster is coming
R ats are scary.

Juwayria Kouser [11]
Manning School for Girls, Aspley

My Birthday

It's my birthday today and I'm so happy
I am 12 years old
I love to play every day
I went to school and did my work
I went home and played with my friends
Then I opened all my presents.

Felicia James (12)
Manning School for Girls, Aspley

My Autumn Poem

It's autumn here
Now the trees are wondering round
The leaves are sizzling down
And the helicopters are whizzing around
The wind is whooshing around
Now everyone have got their coats on
Its shivering cold but here we go
The leaves are coming off the trees.

Toni Sweet (13)
Manning School for Girls, Aspley

Us

I was born there,
And I never moved,
My mum and dad,
I never knew,
I had friends,
But they've gone.
Now I am here,
On my own,
As just an old mushroom
On my own,
But I now have a new special friend,
My girlfriend snail,
Who visits me as soon as she can.

My life is simple,
As can be,
I try to not be crushed,
And I have a family,
That lives up a tree,
We love the rain.
You see I am the snail,
And I am as slow as can be,
Am not good at running
I love everybody,
But my true home is,
With my boyfried mushroom,
On the side of the tree.

I am a tree,
Sad and not so lonely,
I am leafless,
I think I am losing my identity,
Everyone laughs,
The children play away.
But I have one friend,
The fox Lasha,
Who lives in a hole below me.

I am a midnight child of the night,
I sleep quietly to not cause a fright.
I can be hungry,
Need to find something to drink,
A puddle or drain. There can be
Food in the bins
But at the end of the day,
And the morning comes in,
I sleep like a fox under a sad tree.

Veronica McKenna-Sandin (12)
Manning School for Girls, Aspley

Alfie

He lies there and waits
For hours on end, waiting
What's he waiting for,
Dinner or fun?

Is he happy
Is he sad
Is he excited
Or is he mad?

He runs up the garden
As fast as the wind
Barking when someone passes
When someone passes by.

Fraser Carter (13)
Portland Comprehensive School, Worksop

Friends

My friends are nice and kind
They have lots on their mind.
They cheer me up when I'm down,
They dress up like a clown.

They help me with my work
Even when I go berserk.
They help me along the way,
They always know what to say.

When we are all old,
We will remember this story that was told.

Chloe Robson (13)
Portland Comprehensive School, Worksop

Best Friend . . .

She's always there and never not,
She always smiles and talks a lot.
I have trust in her and she has trust in me,
She's my shoulder to cry on you see.

I remember that day up in the woods,
She was a bit merry and wouldn't shut up!
It was actually funny, because we all fell over,
We were rolling down the hill,
That was a night to remember . . .

There was one night when we went to Chesterfield Cinema,
Her brother and friend came and we were running all over!
We watched 'Step Up 3D' and we had a laugh,
Especially on the bus when she was picking up tickets . . .
You do the math;
She's crazy but she's my best friend
And I love her the way she is!

Ashliene Swan (13)
Portland Comprehensive School, Worksop

Shopping

S uper shops
H oping to get everything inside
O pening every shop door to see what's inside
P eeping through windows
P aying at the counter
I ntense running
N ever leave a shop until you've bought something
G lancing through the shops.

Summer Cookson (12)
Portland Comprehensive School, Worksop

My Mother

Mother of all mothers,
A best friend to me.
With all the time sharing,
The love you can't see.

Sometimes you're mad,
Often me to blame.
But sometimes you're sad,
Which makes me feel the same.

Some may dislike,
Some may be lost,
But a mother like you,
Comes at no cost.

Emma Davidson (14)
Portland Comprehensive School, Worksop

Chocolate!

Chocolate is tasty, chocolate is nice,
Whether it tastes of sugar or spice.
When it is filled with strawberry cream,
It sends me off into my own little dream.
When it's an orange crunch
Which everyone likes to munch,
Oh I wish I had one for my lunch.

Kimberley Mace (12)
Portland Comprehensive School, Worksop

Winter's Coming

Winter will soon be here
Happy thoughts and Christmas cheer
Holly berries, mistletoe
All will make our noses glow.

Walking in the freezing snow
Sliding, slipping as we go
Throwing snowballs, having fun
Glad that all our school work's done.

Our dog, Joe, is joining in
How I love to run with him
Making patterns in the snow
Come on Joe, let's go, go, go!

Back home safe and sound
Mum in kitchen, running round
Everyone happy as can be
Full of cheer and Christmas glee.

Winter's coming.

Emily Selby (13)
Portland Comprehensive School, Worksop

Autumn

Leaves fall, twisting, twirling to the ground,
As the wind swirls round and round.

Red, orange and sometimes green,
Are the colours of the autumn leaves.

Scarves and gloves keep me warm,
As I make my way through a leafy swarm.

Autumn colours begin to fade,
As snow starts to fall and takes its place.

Winter has now arrived
But I prefer the autumn time.

Lucy Cairns (13)
Portland Comprehensive School, Worksop

Nature

The beautiful nature swallowed me whole
The glorious breeze that makes me shiver
The tiny thing that looked like a vole
It climbed and weaved across my toes that made me shudder

Nature, what can we do?
Dance and sway till the birds squawk while
All the rabbits have a poo
Shout and sing until the grass grins

Splash! Splash! through the river, giving the fish a fright
Nasty ones biting your toes
It looks as if the foxes have been up all night
But where they have been nobody knows.

Amy Bird (12)
Portland Comprehensive School, Worksop

Untitled

I closed my eyes but I could still see
What was this strangeness happening to me?
I pinch myself and it doesn't hurt
I'm not in a grave, there is no dirt
Nothing looks the same anymore
It's as if I went through and closed the door
I see a strange light up ahead
I cannot stop, I know I'm not dead
The light gets brighter with each minute
I strain to see, there's something in it
Then I see, I cannot swerve
I crash into the car and bounce to the kerb
I lay with broken antennae and wings
There is no way to salvage these things
Win a Mustang GT Convertible or £50,000!
I look up from the road
There before me was a very big toad
Last thing I remember was a sticky tug
Oops! No longer a bug.

Zackary Clarke (12)
Portland Comprehensive School, Worksop

I Love . . .

Happy memories and photographs,
I love the people that make me laugh,
I love all the colours of the rainbow,
I love my phone, I take it everywhere I go,
I love all my family and my friends,
My love for Facebook will never end,
And my pets are my whole world!

Bethany Dobson (12)
Portland Comprehensive School, Worksop

School's Out

I wake up in the morning,
Stretching and yawning.
My curtains are shaking,
I can hear my mum baking.
My eyes are drifting,
The smell of my breakfast lifting.
My mind is skating,
I know the school bus is waiting.
I rush to get ready,
Not wanting to go steady.
I run for the bus,
Get told off because I made a fuss.
I sit bored in all the lessons,
Just listening to all the different questions.
I sit next to my friends at lunch,
Watching them all crunch and munch.
When I go home,
I sit on the bus all alone.
Everyone screams and shouts,
So glad that school's out!

Katie Annable (12)
Portland Comprehensive School, Worksop

The Match

Cup final today,
We've made it all this way.
Fans chanting from their heart,
Hoping our team will have a good start.
As the match begins, the crowd release a roar,
What a shot, after that, we can't really ask for more.
After all this time, score's the same,
He hit a shot with a wicked aim . . . goal!
They were shocked, couldn't believe it,
But for us, the pressure, that'll relieve it!
They've pulled back level,
That shot had the venom of the Devil.
Full time, all square,
No winner, no loser, all to share.
After that, golden goal,
Now players will play from their soul.
Finally, after a while,
We scored a goal that brought a smile.
The full-time whistle sounded.
We're the champs, they got pounded.

Jack Manship (13)
Portland Comprehensive School, Worksop

People

Some people are mardy, some people are smelly,
Some people are bad, some people are mean,
Some people are harsh, some people like jelly,
Some people are fab, some people are clean.

Some people are amazing, some people are crazy,
Some people are wicked, some people are cool,
Some people are funny, some people are lazy,
Some people are great, some people rule.

Some people are friendly, some people are smart,
Some people are awesome, some people like tea,
Some people are great, some people are silly,
Some people are ace, no one else is like me.

Daniel Arnold (12)
Portland Comprehensive School, Worksop

A True Friend

When I see you, you make me smile
You help me go that extra mile

We have our ups, we have our downs
When we're together I never frown

When I'm in a mess you help me out
I've never had any doubts

You'll always be a true friend
I'll love you till the very end.

Katie Wagstaff (12)
Portland Comprehensive School, Worksop

Spring

Out in the open,
In the fresh-scented air,
With pleasure and warmth,
I shout without a care.

With groups of golden daffodils,
Scattered neatly under trees,
Not to mention the attraction of all so many bees.

Hopeful chirps and boisterous birds,
And constant sounds of joy,
A summoned Earth finally awakes,
Discovering the wonder this new day makes.

Lucy Wheatley (13)
Portland Comprehensive School, Worksop

Football

Football, the beautiful game,
He shoots, he misses, what a shame.
The crowd goes wild, Gerald was right good,
I think he is Gerrard's child.
The midfield shot down the wing.
When he's older he will be professional
And have lots of bling.
Three whistles ended the game
We lost 3-1, I got the blame.

Taylor O'Fee (13)
Portland Comprehensive School, Worksop

Jake

I need him more than a flower needs water.
I love him more than Rosie loves Jim.
He makes me smile when I feel down
If I'm upset all I have to do is think of him.

We've had loads of fun memories
And have loads more to come
He makes me feel extremely special.
A lot more than some.

He has amazing sense of fashion
And is my number one favourite footballer.
There is not a single thing you could fault
Only if he creates a drama.

I miss him loads, especially our talks
And watching his footie team on a Sunday.
I also miss him blasting his music
And giggling while he ran for the bus on a Monday.

I love him loads and loads
Especially when he calls me darling.

Ellie Unwin (13)
Portland Comprehensive School, Worksop

Winter Has Arrived

Trees are bare,
Trees are bare,
And the wind is cold and bitter,
The winter clothes are out and tighter.

The robins have arrived
And the snow is falling slow but heavy,
Making a white blanket over the grassy fields.

Trees are bare,
Trees are bare,
We're in December.

The kids are counting the hours and the days
Till they get their visit from St Nicholas.
To the frost scattered on the windows
And the radiators are getting hotter now.

Trees are bare,
Trees are bare,
The wind is cold and bitter.

Who's ready for a warm cup of hot chocolate?

Elise Marshall (13)
Portland Comprehensive School, Worksop

Growing Up

A little child,
With hands so small,
But when he cries his little call,
He needs some help,
A friendly face
To help him walk,
Pace by pace.

He learns to walk
And soon to run,
To chase around,
In the summer sun.
He rides a bike,
With stabilisers on,
But soon enough
They'll all be gone.

The first day of school,
Is a bit of a shock,
But he gets to leave early,
At 1 o'clock!

Mum cries in the playground,
As he waves goodbye,
But she will always love him
And he knows that's why.

Mhairi MacDonald (14)
Portland Comprehensive School, Worksop

When . . .

When the sun is not up
Can it still shine through?
Can it guide you from a place
So dark and blue?

When the morning birds don't sing
Can the morning still begin?
Can the night end
Causing happiness within?

When the Devil stands out
Can the goodness still be shown?
Can a helping hand be given
To those who feel alone?

When your heart breaks
Can you still smile?
Can you get past this pain?
It will only last a while.

When the moon is not whole
Can the man still see?
Can he see the stone-hard passion
Between you and me?

When God cannot be felt
Can the faith be kept?
Can our prayers be savoured
For the mother that wept?

When you're surrounded by tears
Can you still stand straight?
Can you keep the patience?
All you need to do is wait.

Kelly Dudhill (14)
Portland Comprehensive School, Worksop

This Is The Time

My heart it pounds
Rapid, rapid, thump, thump!
A deafening sound
I've got a lump in my throat.

My eyes are prickling
I feel I'm falling.
My past unravelling
I hear the calling.

The luminous light
Dazzling my eyes.
I rise above the others
My time to shine.

Chloe Elwell [13]
Portland Comprehensive School, Worksop

Blackjack

B eautiful pony so, so fun,
L ikes to lay in the sun,
A cts silly in the past,
C anters really, really fast,
K icking the bales of hay,
J ump, dance and play,
A nd he doesn't like sugar mice,
C olours of him are so shiny and nice,
K ing to me, he rules my world!

Emily Shereen Parkin [12]
Portland Comprehensive School, Worksop

My Mum

She's always been there for me through thick or thin,
My nearest of kin,
Through the hard times,
The times of despair,
My best friend till the end.

The good times,
The great,
All of the best lines,
Our laughs and our tears,
Through the best years.

From 0-14,
What a dream,
You always cue the lines,

At the best times!

Thank you Mum.

Alicia Snape (14)
Portland Comprehensive School, Worksop

The Dog Poem

There was a dog on a wall
Who fell on a ball
With shock
He ran off home
To his dome
There he stayed
Till he learned
Not to fall off a wall
On a ball
And to stand up tall.

James Smith (12)
Portland Comprehensive School, Worksop

A Dream

I settle down
Upon my bed,
Without a sound
All words unsaid.

My head is resting
And my dreams are dashing,
Who knows what's next?
The lights are flashing.

Morning is here
And the night is gone,
Even so
Again the night will come.

Liam Hunt (13)
Portland Comprehensive School, Worksop

Food

How hungry I can get.
I'll raid the fridge, you can bet.
A slice of pie, a chunk of meat.
It's all good, I still love to eat.

Danny Seeley (13)
Portland Comprehensive School, Worksop

Memories

Memories; the good, the bad
Some happy and some sad.
Nearest and dearest that have passed
Friendships that you thought would last.

The younger years were the best
Some kind of learning test
Riding a bike, leaning on the wall,
Letting go, hoping not to fall.

Those younger years I miss the most
Idea of fun? Going to the coast.
The thing that hurt the most was a scraped knee,
Biggest achievement - climbing a tree.

I miss the days, everything was easy.
Then I grew up.
Lost friends with silly arguments,
Family members of old age,
But one thing I won't lose?
The memories; they will stay with me forever.

Antonia Oakley (13)
Portland Comprehensive School, Worksop

Untitled

With dirty knees and dungarees,
I made my mark on the walls.
Endless tens, and colouring pens
And tears from a thousand falls.

From place to place without a trace,
I met a million friends . . .
She's packing now, we're gone again
To escape while the cracks mend.

After years and years, he's still here . . .
Apparently it's love?
Confused minds and messed up heads.

That's the word she doesn't know
The meaning of!

Charlotte Robinson (13)
Portland Comprehensive School, Worksop

Misunderstood

Some people follow,
Some people lead,
But I do nothing, I am just me.
You can laugh,
You can tease,
But these shoes, this skirt, they are just me.
I can go away, but come back the same.
I am who I am
And will not change!

Lilly Feeney (13)
Portland Comprehensive School, Worksop

My Auntie Helen

My auntie Helen is very kind,
She is always on my mind.
I think about her night and day,
When I am troubled she helps me find the way.

Her children always help her out,
As she cannot get herself about.
She is very lucky to have them there,
Without them she could not bear.

She calms me down when I am mad,
And holds me tight when I am sad.
Everybody tries to help her in time,
But in my heart I know she is mine.
To love and cherish in my mind forever,
And when I forget? That will be never.

My auntie Helen is in my heart,
I know for sure.
And she will be there,
For evermore.

Bethan Lee [14]
Portland Comprehensive School, Worksop

My Friends

You mean the world
And I am sure
You will be here
For evermore.

You're there beside me
Through thick and thin
With you my friends
I always win.

So thank you friends
For being there
With you my secrets
I always share.

Every day together
Is one I will hold
Forever in my heart
And when I'm grey and old.

Jaycee Dickson (13)
Portland Comprehensive School, Worksop

My Poem

I'm in the dingy dark room,
It is silent,
Thinking how I'll be out there soon.

The room is full,
We all stand up together,
As we walk out, the sky is dull,
It's terrible weather.

Every step I take I dig my studs in,
Just to get comfy,
We're at the city of sins,
Away at Liverpool.

This is a rivalry nobody forgets,
All the fans want you to do
Is put the ball in the back of the net.

Christopher O'Grady (14)
Portland Comprehensive School, Worksop

My Safe Haven

That small little town called home,
Is not mine anymore,
I can't call it my own.

My perfect little house,
So safe and sound,
Has been smashed
And smothered to the ground.

And all those memories
Trapped in those walls,
Have been lost forever,
I've lost them all.

All those people that were close to me,
They've drifted all away,
And ever since I've left that place,
It's never been the same.

I had a special, happy life,
I tried to run away from fresh starts,
But I got plunged into the unknown,
And ended up hurting my heart.

I miss my safe little haven,
And everything I used to be,
The things I cherish, hold the most,
That meant the most to me.

Imana Panezai (13)
Portland Comprehensive School, Worksop

Beloved Brother

Brother, oh brother
With the bright green eyes
Which light up I see
Like the sun in its sky

You do crack some jokes
Makes me laugh out loud.
Your personality is great
Of which I'm proud.

That you're my brother
I'm so glad you are
You've done so much for me
I know you'll go far.

Katy Tindle (14)
Portland Comprehensive School, Worksop

Follow My Dreams

Just because I say I love you
It doesn't mean you can push me around
You use me and bruise me and lie through your teeth
But those three words don't mean I should take it
You control me and I hate it
You play me like a puppet on a string
But this heart beats for you . . .
Please don't break it
Let me free and let me . . .
Follow my dreams.

Louise Stuart (13)
Portland Comprehensive School, Worksop

Untitled

I love him,
His eyes, his hair, I love him.
His perfect skin, the cute smile,
I love him, look in his sparkling eyes,
I love him.

He bought me roses, smelled so sweet.
I hugged him and smiled, I love him.
His laugh is annoying but sexy too,
I love him.

He treats me like a princess
And he acts like a prince.
He can make a good Sunday dinner,
I love him, I love him, I love him.

I feel so weak, he broke my heart.
He crushed me, how will I live?
I loved him!

Victoria Page (14)
Portland Comprehensive School, Worksop

My Hamsters

My hamsters are like a cheetah
Prowling through the grass
They always smile at some glass
And they laugh like a hyena can
When they run in a golden tin can.

Nathan Hancock (11)
Portland Comprehensive School, Worksop

Twilight

T wilight is the best
E specially Edward and the rest
A moment of never-ending love
M aybe I'll see him one day

E dward is the best
D o get rid of all the rest
W hat would I do without him there?
A cuddle every moment of the day
R eset time so this will never end
D reaming of the day.

Megan Neilan (13)
Portland Comprehensive School, Worksop

Football

Football is my life
Pass, shoot and score
I always want more

I have several best friends
All legends
All staying till the end

My mum, dad and baby brother
All amazing
And one's called Reggie.

Charlie Shelton (13)
Portland Comprehensive School, Worksop

Island Of Fun

The sun's shining on my face,
The wind blowing past my face,
We're having a race,
Across the beach.

Animals playing,
Birds back-flipping,
Parrots saying,
'Hello, hello!'

Danny Ashmore (13)
Portland Comprehensive School, Worksop

You, My Friend

You, my friend, are dear to me,
When I am sad, I want you near to me.
When everything around me seems vile,
You are the one who can make me smile.

You, my friend, are amazing,
You end up every day, raising
My hopes and my moods,
And you seldom snigger at me if I lose.

You, my friend, are so funny,
You can make all of my days sunny,
If the teacher catches me giggling,
You were the one who was singing!

You, my friend, are dear to me,
I hope you'll never drift away from me,
You're amazing, funny and sweet,
And I'm very glad that we did meet!

Elina Bennett (13)
Portland Comprehensive School, Worksop

Featured Poets:
DEAD POETS
AKA Mark Grist & MC Mixy

Mark Grist and MC Mixy joined forces to become the 'Dead Poets' in 2008.

Since then Mark and Mixy have been challenging the preconceptions of poetry and hip hop across the country. As 'Dead Poets', they have performed in venues ranging from nightclubs to secondary schools; from festivals to formal dinners. They've appeared on Radio 6 Live with Steve Merchant, they've been on a national tour with Phrased and Confused and debuted their show at the 2010 Edinburgh Fringe, which was a huge success.

Both Mark and Mixy work on solo projects as well as working together as the 'Dead Poets'. Both have been Peterborough's Poet Laureate, with Mixy holding the title for 2010.

The 'Dead Poets' are available for workshops in your school as well as other events. Visit www.deadpoetry.co.uk for further information and to contact the guys!

Read on to pick up some fab writing tips!

Your
WORKSHOPS

In these workshops we are going to look at writing styles and examine some literary techniques that the 'Dead Poets' use. Grab a pen, and let's go!

Rhythm Workshop

Rhythm in writing is like the beat in music. Rhythm is when certain words are produced more forcefully than others, and may be held for longer duration. The repetition of a pattern is what produces a 'rhythmic effect'. The word rhythm comes from the Greek meaning of 'measured motion'.

Count the number of syllables in your name. Then count the number of syllables in the following line, which you write in your notepad: 'My horse, my horse, will not eat grass'.

Now, highlight the longer sounding syllables and then the shorter sounding syllables in a different colour.

Di dum, di dum, di dum, di dum is a good way of summing this up.

You should then try to write your own lines that match this rhythm. You have one minute to see how many you can write!

Examples include:
'My cheese smells bad because it's hot'
and
'I do not like to write in rhyme'.

For your poem, why don't you try to play with the rhythm? Use only longer beats or shorter beats? Create your own beat and write your lines to this?

Did you know ... ?

Did you know that paper was invented in China around 105AD by Ts'ai Lun. The first English paper mill didn't open until 1590 and was in Dartford.

Rhyme Workshop

Start off with the phrase 'I'd rather be silver than gold' in your notepad. and see if you can come up with lines that rhyme with it -
'I'd rather have hair than be bald'
'I'd rather be young than be old'
'I'd rather be hot than cold'
'I'd rather be bought than sold'

Also, pick one of these words and see how many rhymes you can find:

Rose

Wall

Warm

Danger

What kinds of rhymes did you come up with? Are there differences in rhymes? Do some words rhyme more cleanly than others? Which do you prefer and why?

Lists Workshop

Game - you (and you can ask your friends or family too) to write as many reasons as possible for the following topics:

Annoying things about siblings

The worst pets ever

The most disgusting ingredients for a soup you can think of

Why not try writing a poem with the same first 2, 3 or 4 words?

I am ...

Or

I love it when ...

Eg:

I am a brother

I am a listener

I am a collector of secrets

I am a messer of bedrooms.

Onomatopoeia Workshop

Divide a sheet of A4 paper into 8 squares.

You then have thirty seconds to draw/write what could make the following sounds:

Splash	Ping
Drip	Bang
Rip	Croak
Crack	Splash

Now try writing your own ideas of onomatopoeia. Why might a writer include onomatopoeia in their writing?

Repetition Workshop

Come up with a list of words/phrases, aim for at least 5. You now must include one of these words in your piece at least 6 times. You aren't allowed to place these words/phrases at the beginning of any of the lines.

Suggested words/phrases:

Why

Freedom

Laughing

That was the best day ever

I can't find the door

I'm in trouble again

The best

Workshop
POETRY 101

Below is a poem written especially for poetry Matters, by MC Mixy. Why not try and write some more poems of your own?

What is Matter?

© MC Mixy

What matters to me may not be the same things that matter to you
You may not agree with my opinion mentality or attitude
The order in which I line up my priorities to move
Choose to include my view and do what I do due to my mood
And state of mind
I make the time to place the lines on stacks of paper and binds
Concentrate on my artwork hard I can't just pass and scrape behind
Always keep close mates of mine that make things right
And even those who can't … just cos I love the way they can try
What matters to me is doing things the right way
It's tough this game of life we play what we think might stray from what others might say
In this world of individuality we all wanna bring originality
Live life and drift through casually but the vicious reality is
Creativity is unique
Opinions will always differ but if you figure you know the truth, speak
So many things matter to me depending on how tragically deep you wanna go
I know I need to defy gravity on this balance beam
As I laugh and breathe draft and read map the scene practise piece smash the beat and graphic release
Visual and vocal it's a standard procedure
Have to believe and don't bite the hand when it feeds ya

If you wanna be a leader you need to stay out of the pen where the sheep are
The things that matter to me are
My art and my friends
That will stay from the start to the end
People will do things you find hard to amend
Expect the attacks and prepare you gotta be smart to defend
I put my whole heart in the blend the mass is halved yet again
I'm marked by my pen a big fish fighting sharks of men
In a small pond
Dodging harpoons and nets hooks and predators tryna dismember ya
I won't let them I won't get disheartened I can fend for myself
As long as I'm doing what's important
I'm my mind where I'm supported is a just cause to be supporting
In these appalling hard times I often find myself falling when
Only two aspects of my life keep me sane and allow me to stand tall again
Out of all of them two is a small number
It's a reminder I remind ya to hold necessity and let luxury fall under
Try to avoid letting depression seep through
Take the lesson we actually need a lot less than we think we do
So what matters to you?
They may be similar to things that matter to me
I'm actually lacking the need of things I feel would help me to succeed
Though I like to keep it simple, I wanna love, I wanna breed
I'm one of many individuals in this world where importance fluctuates and varies
Things that matter will come and go
But the ones that stay for long enough must be worth keeping close
If you're not sure now don't watch it you'll know when you need to know
Me, I think I know now … yet I feel and fear I don't.

Turn overleaf for a poem by Mark Grist and some fantastic hints and tips!

Workshop
POETRY 101

What Tie Should I Wear Today?

© Mark Grist

I wish I had a tie that was suave and silk and slick,
One with flair, that's debonair and would enchant with just one flick,
Yeah, I'd like that … a tie that's hypnotizing,
I'd be very restrained and avoid womanising,
But all the lady teachers would still say 'Mr Grist your tie's so charming!'
As I cruise into their classrooms with it striking and disarming.
At parents' evenings my tie's charm would suffice,
In getting mums to whisper as they leave 'Your English teacher seems nice!'

Or maybe an evil-looking tie - one that's the business,
Where students will go 'Watch out! Mr Grist is
on the prowl with that evil tie.'
The one that cornered Josh and then ripped out his eye.
Yeah no one ever whispers, no one ever sniggers,
Or my tie would rear up and you'd wet your knickers.
Maybe one girl just hasn't heard the warning,
Cos she overslept and turned up late to school that morning,
And so I'd catch her in my lesson yawning … oh dear.
I'd try to calm it down, but this tie's got bad ideas.
It'd size the girl up and then just as she fears,
Dive in like a serpent snapping at her ears.
There'd be a scream, some blood and lots and lots of tears,
And she wouldn't be able to yawn again for years.

Or maybe … a tie that everyone agrees is mighty fine
And people travel from miles around to gawp at the design
I'd like that … a tie that pushes the boundaries of tieware right up to the limit
It'd make emos wipe their tears away while chavs say 'It's wicked innit?'
and footy lads would stop me with 'I'd wear that if I ever won the cup.'
And I'd walk through Peterborough to slapped backs, high fives, thumbs up
While monosyllabic teenagers would just stand there going 'Yup.'

I don't know. I'd never be sure which of the three to try
As any decision between them would always end a tie.

130

Tips and Advice for
PERFORMING
Your Poem

So you've written your poem, now how about performing it.
Whether you read your poem for the first time in front of your class, school or strangers at an open mic event or poetry slam, these tips will help you make the best of your performance.

Breathe and try to relax.

Every poet that reads in front of people for the first time feels a bit nervous, when you're there you are in charge and nothing serious can go wrong.

People at poetry slams or readings are there to support the poets. They really are!

If you can learn your poem off by heart that is brilliant, however having a piece of paper or notebook with your work in is fine, though try not to hide behind these.

It's better to get some eye contact with the audience.
If you're nervous find a friendly face to focus on.

Try to read slowly and clearly and enjoy your time in the spotlight.

Don't rush up to the microphone, make sure it's at the right height for you and if you need it adjusted ask one of the team around you.

Before you start, stand up as straight as you can and get your body as comfortable as you can and remember to hold your head up.

The microphone can only amplify what what's spoken into it; if you're very loud you might end up deafening people and if you only whisper or stand too far away you won't be heard.

When you say something before your poem, whether that's hello or just the title of your poem, try and have a listen to how loud you sound. If you're too quiet move closer to the microphone, if you're too loud move back a bit.

Remember to breathe! Don't try to say your poem so quickly you can't find time to catch your breath.

And finally, **enjoy!**

Poetry FACTS

Here are a selection of fascinating poetry facts!

No word in the English language rhymes with 'MONTH'.

William Shakespeare was born on 23rd April 1564 and died on 23rd April 1616.

The haiku is one of the shortest forms of poetic writing.
Originating in Japan, a haiku poem is only seventeen syllables, typically broken down into three lines of five, seven and five syllables respectively.

The motto of the Globe Theatre was 'totus mundus agit histrionem' (the whole world is a playhouse).

The Children's Laureate award was an idea by Ted Hughes and Michael Morpurgo.

The 25th January each year is Burns' Night, an occasion in honour of Scotland's national poet Robert Burns.

Spike Milligan's 'On the Ning Nang Nong' was voted the UK's favourite comic poem in 1998.

Did you know *onomatopoeia* means the word you use sounds like the word you are describing – like the rain *pitter-patters* or the snow *crunches* under my foot.

'Go' is the shortest complete sentence in the English language.

Did you know rhymes were used in olden days to help people remember the news? Ring-o'-roses is about the Plague!

The Nursery Rhyme 'Old King Cole' is based on a real king and a real historical event. King Cole is supposed to have been an actual monarch of Britain who ruled around 200 A.D.

Edward Lear popularised the limerick with his poem 'The Owl and the Pussy-Cat'.

Lewis Carroll's poem 'The Jabberwocky' is written in nonsense style.

POEM – noun

1. a composition in verse, esp. one that is characterized by a highly developed artistic form and by the use of heightened language and rhythm to express an intensely imaginative interpretation of the subject.

Poetry TIPS

We have compiled some helpful tips for you budding poets...

In order to write poetry, read lots of poetry!

Keep a notebook with you at all times so you can write whenever (and wherever) inspiration strikes.

Every line of a poem should be important to the poem and interesting to read. A poem with only 3 great lines should be 3 lines long.

Use an online rhyming dictionary to improve your vocabulary.

Use free workshops and help sheets to learn new poetry styles.

Experiment with visual patterns - does your written poetry create a good pattern on the page?

Try to create pictures in the reader's mind - aim to fire the imagination.

Develop your voice. Become comfortable with how you write.

Listen to criticism, and try to learn from it, but don't live or die by it.

Say what you want to say, let the reader decide what it means.

Notice what makes other's poetry memorable. Capture it, mix it up and make it your own. (Don't copy other's work word for word!)

Go wild. Be funny. Be serious. Be whatever you want!

Grab hold of something you feel - anything you feel - and write it.

The more you write, the more you develop. Write poetry often.

Use your imagination, your own way of seeing.

Feel free to write a bad poem, it will develop your 'voice'.

Did you know ...?

'The Epic of Gilgamesh' was written thousands of years ago in Mesopotamia and is the oldest poem on record.

134

Family

A silver sheet over reality,
Happiness over sad,
Smiles over utter despair,
Good over bad.

Words over feelings,
Lies over truths,
Sanity over craziness,
Me over you.

Secrets hidden,
Buried deep,
Thoughts not to remember,
Memories not to keep.

Places not to go,
People not to see,
Values didn't matter,
Not even family.

A perfect, pure disaster,
A tear from an eye,
A flood of anger,
A heartbreaking sigh.

A cold emotion,
A cold inside,
A cold remembrance,
A cold goodbye.

Blackness in the future,
Guarding the past,
No one to tell,
From everyone, to keep back.

Nothing to defend,
Nothing to share,
Never a love,
Never a care.

Bella Tennant (13)
Portland Comprehensive School, Worksop

My Light In The Dark

A figure stands in front of me,
Higher than the clouds,
The thing I will aspire to be,
To the figure I bowed.

I stand here today,
With a smile on my face,
Always great; that's your way,
Higher than space.

As I look up to the sun,
I look up to you too,
There was a battle and I won,
All because of you.

You're the reason I live,
For you I'd die,
You're the reason I love, love, love,
The reason I won't cry, cry, cry.

When things get tough,
I look up to you,
It isn't enough,
I mirror the things you do.

You're the reason I will make something
Of the life I live,
For you I will do something,
You inspired me to give.

Rachael Bartrop (13)
Portland Comprehensive School, Worksop

Alone

Sat alone in the corner,
The world flashes by,
People don't notice me,
I start to cry.

Children laugh at me,
They point and stare,
I start to think,
People don't care.

Why, why, why does this happen to me?
Why, why, why can't people see?
Why, why, why does nobody care?
Why, why, why is there nobody there?

I stagger to my weary feet,
Men and women bump into me,
I walk across the cobbles and rocks,
I'm as distraught as can be.

Why smile in the shining sun,
When no one gives a damn?
I sit on a bench and realise,
No one is as lonely as I am!

Hannah Sinnott (13)
Portland Comprehensive School, Worksop

Seasons

The wonders of winter, a chill in the air.
Frost in the morning and snow everywhere.
Trees silhouetted against dusky skies,
Chocolates and cakes, not forgetting mince pies.

Signs of spring emerge from the ground,
Sprouting leaves, young birds all around.
Dawn chorus at the break of day,
Newborn animals out at play.

The scorching sunshine, summer arrives.
Bees gather nectar to take to their hives.
The kids are excited, six weeks of no school,
The parents exhausted, relax by the pool.

Arrays of autumn colours abound,
As crispy leaves cascade to the ground.
Foggy mornings and days of rain,
Darker evenings bring winter again.

Thomas Askwith (13)
Portland Comprehensive School, Worksop

What Matters To Me?

Ambitions in life are easy to dream
But hard to follow.
People who never give up and keep trying are survivors.

Music to me means everything I could wish for.
You would never think it could help you when you need help the most.
Each song has a reason for everything and a reason for you and me.

Friends and family I'll guess not every family member I'm close to,
But the ones that are there for me, I guess I love them and friends.
If it weren't for them I wouldn't be who I would be today.

Conchita Foster (12)
Portland Comprehensive School, Worksop

My Poem

Games are what I like to play,
Games can make me quietly dismay.
They make me joyful, they make me sad,
Sometimes I even get quite mad.

Sports are what I like to play,
Sports can make me feel so grey.
I am sometimes bad, but mostly great,
When I do well I don't dictate.

David Colton (14)
Portland Comprehensive School, Worksop

Untitled

I'm a runner
I'm a jumper
I'm a flyer
I'm a dyer

I'm a spinner
I'm a winner
I'm a survivor
I'm a scuba diver

I'm a fighter
I'm a smiter
I'm a crazy
I'm a lazy.

Callum Furey (12)
Portland Comprehensive School, Worksop

Leaves Of Love

The autumn leaves crunch beneath my feet,
The taste in the air, sour but sweet,
I see a ditch so over it I leap,
But land in another so terribly deep,
Up I jump as fast as I can,
That's when I feel someone take my hand,
Who could this loving stranger be?
That's when I realise he knows me,
It's the boy from down my street,
What a coincidence that here we meet,
Off we run towards the trees,
Don't let me forget this moment please,
He tells me that he's leaving town,
This makes me want to tumble down,
Before he goes he looks me in the eye,
That's when I know this isn't our last goodbye.

Ellen Pedley (12)
Portland Comprehensive School, Worksop

The Island

Cold breeze on my face,
Not a peep throughout the place.
Sea, sand and sights, everywhere you look,
Bushes were shaking and the tree branches shook.
The big blue sea rippled on the beach,
Coconuts in the tree but far out of reach.

James Merrills (13)
Portland Comprehensive School, Worksop

My Poetry

Football . . . football,
That's the life for me,
Football . . . football,
That's the place to be.

Xbox . . . Xbox,
That's the life for me,
Xbox . . . Xbox,
That's the game to be.

Food . . . food,
That's the pizza for me,
Food . . . food,
That's the sensation to be.

Life . . . life,
That's the best thing for me,
Life . . . life,
That's the life to be.

Adam Wake (14)
Portland Comprehensive School, Worksop

Flowers

Flowers in bloom,
Throughout June,
Lots of wild daisies,
Making little ant mazes.

Sunflowers tall
And pansies small,
Flowers, we love them all.

Honeysuckle for the bees,
And the birds in the trees,
Water irises near the pond,
Oh I am so fond
Of flowers growing in the summer.

Eleanor Wilkinson (13)
Portland Comprehensive School, Worksop

I Love My Sister

My little sister can be . . .
Angry, annoying, crazy and loud - she is!
But I love my sister.

My little sister should be . . .
Amusing, calm, relaxed and quiet - she's not!
But I love my sister!

My little sister is very much . . .
Absurd, affectionate, loud, loveable and tiny,
That's why I love my sister immensely.

Alix Wood (14)
Portland Comprehensive School, Worksop

My Favourite Day

When I do my rapping, my beat's so sweet
When the girls look at me, they're like birds going tweet, tweet
Then I go and dance and spin on my head
I get so dizzy that I need to lay on my bed.

I play football on a Sunday morning
When we're winning ten-nil it gets kinda boring
At the end of the match when I score the awesome winner
Then I come home for my tasty Sunday dinner.

For the final hour I read my book
Then I wind my mum up by calling her 'Duck',
The next day I get ready for school
But I don't even obey all the main rules!

Mason Gee (11)
Portland Comprehensive School, Worksop

Football Poem

F ootball is the game to play
O ffside is one of the rules of the day
O n the pitch
T eams try their best
B ut it's not that easy to get it in the back of the net
A t ninety minutes the whistle will blow
L eaving one team on a high
L eaving one team on a low.

Megan Edwards (11)
Portland Comprehensive School, Worksop

Winter

The cold winter's air
Blows swiftly through my hair,
When the wind blows the trees
It feels as if you are going to freeze.

As the rain starts to fall,
The puddles become bigger,
The grass becomes tall
And looks like a figure.

As the dark nights close in
The cold frost fills the ground,
You hope the snow is coming
But you don't know until it's found.

The Christmas season is near
As the snowflakes appear.
You know that Christmas Day
Will soon be here.

Emma Levitt (13)
Portland Comprehensive School, Worksop

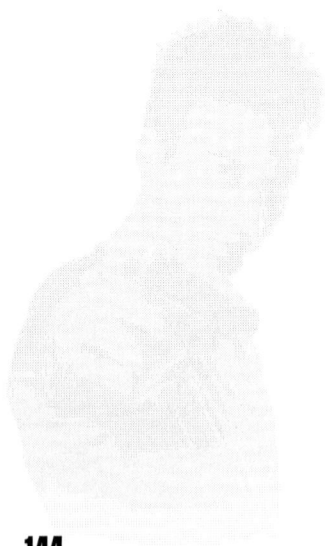

Music Matters

Music is important to me
It's like salt in the sea
It's just meant to be
Without music life's pointless to me

Music is like a drug
It can take away the pain
It can make people forget
With every note that is played

Music is the one thing
That is there till the end
When everyone else is busy
Music never dies

Music is amazing
It will be when I'm sat in a rocking chair
With greying hair
Helping me through the days.

Levi Richardson (14)
Portland Comprehensive School, Worksop

What Matters To Me?

Maryanne matters so much to me, she's like a sister.
Amber, an amazing friend who always makes you smile.
Time I wrote about not just friends who are like sisters but other things.
Every day is important as I'm spending it with people I love.
Sheridan, this is me, a friendly person.
I'm the kindest, loudest person you will meet.
Amazingly I always want to be a singer or actress,
But for now I'll be a drama queen.
Really reminding me of my happy memories,
There are special photos all around me.
Ellie W, another one of my BFFs,
She's the one who gives me the support and comfort I need.
Family, the most important thing to me, the important thing in my life.
Agony there may be, but it's like a plane,
We crash but somehow always manage to stick together.
Making friends all of the time,
I'll find more good mates but not as good as Maryanne.
I'll always be there if you need me
Because that's the type of person I am.
Love me if you're my mate
But if you don't then you can't be a true friend.
You always know what matters to you.

Sheridan Hoyle (12)
Portland Comprehensive School, Worksop

What Matters To Me?

Well that's simple. It's friends, it's the friendship
that never ends . . .

It's the way they love and care for you,
and pick you up when you fall.
It's the way they cheer you up,
and come for you when you call.

It's the way they make you feel much better,
and are always there for you.
It's the way they stick up for you no matter what,
and tell you secrets you never knew.

When you give them a hug,
and you're filled with warmness and love.
When you argue and shout,
because that's what it's about.

When you need a hand and they're always there,
when they have sweets and they will always share.
When you're told that you're loved,
when you're not pushed and shoved.
It gives you a glow, that just goes to show,
friendship means everything.

Stephanie Oakes (12)
Portland Comprehensive School, Worksop

What Music Means To Me . . .

As I step from the darkness into the light,
Like waking from slumber - coming from night,
Bright lights glare my vision but I can still see,
Expressionless faces staring at me.

I sit down in front of the piano so wide,
With nowhere to run to, nowhere to hide,
I rest my fingers on the ivory keys,
Silence falls like going from rough to calm seas.

I begin to play but my mind still lingers,
A rainbow cloth flows beneath my fingers,
A glimmer of hope, the spark of a dream,
All around me faces gleam.

But when I'm finished I'm met by applause,
People smile right at me, and of course,
A smile on my face stretches from ear to ear,
Because I love my music, it wipes away fear.

Katy Lambkin (12)
Portland Comprehensive School, Worksop

Newcastle United

In the crowd people pushing,
In the queue people rushing,
To our seats we ran,
Sat down and the game began.

The Magpies are winning, a rush inside,
If it stays like this I will burst with pride.

'Toon, Toon, black and white army,
Toon, Toon, black and white army,'
The Geordies chant.

The end of the match,
Score was 2-0,
What a great result,
Now we are though.

Today was the best,
Me and my friend
Will remember this right till the end.

Chloe Pickering (13)
Portland Comprehensive School, Worksop

My Poem

I am new to this school,
So far I think it is quite cool,
I have met new friends,
They all have different trends!

My favourite lesson so far,
Is learning to play the guitar,
I am having lessons you see,
I think it's cool would you agree?

The thing I like the most,
I don't want to boast,
Is to have our lessons I have to go,
To different classrooms (weird, I know)

But even though I like this place,
Somewhere there's a sad smile on my face,
I miss my primary school a little,
Even though it was a bit brittle.

Anyway I am done,
But I've had lots of fun,
Writing poems I think is nice,
I write them every day (well, once or twice).

Emily Harlington (12)
Portland Comprehensive School, Worksop

Paige Mountain

Food, food, food,
What tasty food,
It's scrumptious yet yummy,
It tickles my tummy

And makes my taste buds explode,
Yet the sensation makes me cry for more,
Oops, I spilt some on the floor,
Oh why, why, why?

My stomach was full again,
I looked outside, it began to rain,
I carried on eating my chilli,
Then I went to see my cousin, Milley.

Paige Mountain (11)
Portland Comprehensive School, Worksop

It Matters To Me!

W orksop, cos that's where I live,
H ome, I got my family in it,
A lex Thorpe, he means a lot, but now he sadly lives in Australia,
T ea, because I like my food.

M SN because I speak to my mates,
A lex used to play footy with me,
T ime to play on Xbox,
T yler's a mate but he supports Sheffield United,
E ngland, because that's my country,
R eading because it sends me to sleep,
S heffield Wednesday, because that's my team.

T ommy Miller, he's my fave player,
O MG, it's time for bed.

M attie Mellor, he's from my old school,
E ngland, we need to up our game in sport.

Jamie Heeley (11)
Portland Comprehensive School, Worksop

Memories

M is for my family who I've had some great times with.
E is for everyone in my school who looked out for me.
M is for my mum who without I would never have learnt to ride a bike.
O is for opening my picture album and looking at the happy and sad times.
R is for relatives who helped me through hard times.
I is for illnesses I've had, I always have people to comfort me.
E is for everyone in my family who I will love for ever and always.
S is for school where I learnt many things
    but most of all I have made the best friends anyone could have!

Beckie Annable (12)
Portland Comprehensive School, Worksop

What Matters To Me?

Family is the world to me,
I see them every day.
I keep them close to me,
They are always in my heart,
It will stay that way.

My sisters are the closest to me,
I always mess around with them,
They are very special to me,
I keep them close beside me,
Every single day.

Every day I think of them
And I miss them all the time,
I don't know what I would do without them,
So let's just hope we stay that way,
Close together forever.

Sian Allsop (13)
Portland Comprehensive School, Worksop

Friends

You're like the wind, blowing through my hair.
You're sometimes so annoying, but I do care.
I know you think that I hate you, but I don't.
We have our fights all the time,
But I won't leave your side if you won't.

We also have some great memories, which I don't want to forget.
I know we have our differences, but I'll always be there, you can bet!
I'll never leave your side, because you're such a good friend.
So put the past behind, live life to the fullest,
And hope this friendship will never end.

Jade Brunt (14)
Portland Comprehensive School, Worksop

Broken Heart

On a cold winter's night in front of the fireplace
The kids holding a picture of their mum close to their face.
Tears start to run down everyone's cheek,
All six of us too sad to speak.
We wish we had appreciated her when she was here
Instead of demanding toys and me shouting, 'More beer!'

Me sitting here and missing her so,
Won't bring her back and with the kids it's all go.
Pictures of happy times on the wall, wedding day photos,
Pictures of the kids learning to crawl,
They were the happy times which no longer remain
But she would have wanted just the same.

A few months later we have began to move on,
Still remembering the motherly figure that has now gone,
The kids now have a smile on their face,
They are proud of their mum
Which they show in their grace.

We have set up a charity in my wife's name,
Stars have given money
That belong there with the fame.
I tell the kids she is the brightest star in the sky
And she will look down with tears in her eye.

She will be proud, happy and so
Why was she the one that had to go?
But as they say that life goes on
The wonderful mum that now will always be gone.

Claire Holloway (13)
Portland Comprehensive School, Worksop

C And F Poem

My name starts with a 'C' and my age starts with an 'F'
Christopher! That's what everyone calls me
I grew, grew and grew up
When I was six years old I had lost one dear in my family
And he went to the glowy Heaven!
I grew, grew and grew up with my wonderful dear mum!
There's never enough love!
Always wish that I could be on a different planet
So we will never lose our loved ones.
My name starts with a 'C' and my age starts with an 'F'
I'm beautifully deaf!

Christopher Probert (15)
Royal School for the Deaf, Derby

Poor Poppy

At Christmas, I bought a hamster called Poppy.
She was cute as whiskers on a kitty.
She was Syrian and she has golden fur on her.
Almost like a dog.
Those eyes are as sparkling as a twinkly star!

One day, she was 1½ years old,
Something bad happened to her,
She was dying like a turtle.
We put her in a soft, cotton, warm bed as in Heaven,
Her heart beat was slow like hiking to the mountain.

Now she's gone to Heaven like an angel,
You belonged to me,
We hope you will have a good time
And we hope you will come back soon . . .
RIP Poppy.

Calum Daly (12)
Royal School for the Deaf, Derby

Pleading Voices

Pleading voices
Tearful eyes
I hope they never see
Through my lies
It won't hurt me
It'll only hurt you
Maybe one day
I'll act as you do
I'll be perfect
And free
My home will be misery
In control
Now that's the goal
Please don't try and see
Inside my soul
It's tainted and impure
The voice in my head
Holds a cure.

Shannice Thompson (13)
St John Houghton Catholic School, Kirk Hallam

Firework Night

Crash! Bang! Whoosh!
The sound of fireworks as they take flight,
The excitement and enjoyment of firework night!

Giggle! Chatter! Eek!
The sound of children playing,
Whilst fireworks are spraying.

Shout! Cheer! Roar!
The sound of adults partying,
Whilst fireworks are crackling.

Clink! Hiccup! Splash!
The sound of wine being poured,
Whilst little children are adored.

Hiss! Crackle! Swoosh!
The sound of the fire being lit,
Whilst the crowds gather round, if they can fit.

Sizzle! Murmur! Bing!
The sound of food coming out,
Whilst children wonder what all the hustle is about!

Megan Arundel (11)
St John Houghton Catholic School, Kirk Hallam

A Journey To Forget

Honk! A car horn went off somewhere,
Anywhere, I wished with all my heart,
Anywhere but here.

Screech! A car made a sudden brake somewhere,
This journey was everlasting,
It wasn't fair.

Argh! My dad growled at someone, somewhere,
We weren't even going somewhere nice,
The thought agitated me.

Plop! I heard a silent tear drop delicately onto my hand,
I didn't want to go to Mum's funeral,
But I had to be strong.

For her . . .

Phoebe Collingridge (11)
St John Houghton Catholic School, Kirk Hallam

The Pet Shop

Baa, baa went the sheep
Zzz, zzz as they went to sleep.
Scuttle, scuttle went the rat
Miaow, miaow cried the cat
Moo, moo went the cow
The owner said, 'Shh now.'
Woof, woof went the dog
As it went bleugh, bleugh down the bog
Squeak, squeak went the mouse
As it scurried to its tiny house.

Kai Grant (12)
St John Houghton Catholic School, Kirk Hallam

The Farm

Cock-a-doodle-doo went the cockerel, waking me up.
Out on the farm, the chickens began to cluck.
The dogs began to bark, the cows began to moo,
And still, the cockerel went cock-a-doodle-doo!
The sheep started to baa, the cats started to miaow.
Oink, oink, oink went the pigs,
Quack, quack, quack went the ducks,
And still, the cockerel went cock-a-doodle-doo!
The horse began to neigh when I arrived,
And the rabbit began to poo.
Then all was quiet,
Apart from the cockerel going cock-a-doodle-doo!

Chloe Bowmar (11)
St John Houghton Catholic School, Kirk Hallam

The Heavy Rain Storm

Pitter-patter goes the rain
Making someone's journey quite a pain,
Whoosh! goes the wind pushing the rain,
I thought this was the main,
Swish! Swish and wash! It sounded quite posh,
Swish, go the cars, it was like driving through Mars,
There was the plane it will never look the same,
Splash! Splash! It came down in a flash
Now there's more, it was hardcore.

Tom Andrews (11)
St John Houghton Catholic School, Kirk Hallam

The Fair

Clank!
Goes the rides being set up.
Bang!
Bash and bump
Go the bumper cars.
Whoosh!
Goes the waltzer
Spinning around.
Giggle
Go the children
Running around.
Sizzle!
Go the sausages
In the catering van.

Amy Morley (11)
St John Houghton Catholic School, Kirk Hallam

The Woods

Woah, woah
went the wind.

Snap, snap
went the twigs.

Whoosh, whoosh
went the trees.

Tu-whit tu-whoo
went the owls.

Chirp, chirp
went the crickets.

Shh, shh
silence came.

Amber Smith (11)
St John Houghton Catholic School, Kirk Hallam

Horse Of The Year Show

Thud, thud go the horse's hooves,
beating on the ground, like a heartbeat.
Snort goes the spooky horse
bucking off the rider.
Ooh, ouch goes the audience
as she lands on the hard, wooden poles of the showjump . . .
Plunk, plunk, plunk go the three poles,
crashing onto the soft sand beneath them.
Crash, as the rider lands on the floor.
And ding-ding goes the bell for the next horse
to take its turn in the ring.
Clap, clap, clap goes the audience
with a smile on their faces.
The horse and rider got a clear round.

Rachel Tooley (11)
St John Houghton Catholic School, Kirk Hallam

Fireworks

Bang, bang, they flew into the air.
Bang, bang, they explode in the night sky.
Clap, clap, children enjoy the scenes.
Sizzle, sizzle, the sausages burn on the barbecue.
Boom, boom, more fireworks fly into the stars.

Joshua Axe (11)
St John Houghton Catholic School, Kirk Hallam

Fireworks

Crash, bang, there they go
Into the sky where nobody knows
Whoosh, they come crashing down
Little children with a frown
The neighbours trying to sleep
But no luck with the bang and creek
Fireworks, fireworks in the sky
Bash, crash and whoosh
With a big smile.

Mitchell Wood (11)
St John Houghton Catholic School, Kirk Hallam

Fireworks Night

Fizz goes the firework as it flutters to the ground.
Plop! go the mushy peas as they are served to people with very cold knees!
Screech go the screamers as they fly above my head into the midnight sky.
Clap! go the hands of people who murmur amongst their own icy breath.
Squish! is the sound of the feet, of many people who chatter amongst us.
Boom! goes the biggest firework to finish off the night.
Then comes a crackle, the guy has arrived!
He's set on fire, with a sizzle, luckily his eyes didn't drizzle.

Charlotte Bird (11)
St John Houghton Catholic School, Kirk Hallam

Stormy Sea

Crack went the lightning,
Splash went the waves,
The cracking and splashing got louder,
As the storm came.

Whoosh went the twister,
Thump went the boat,
As it kept hitting the waves,
Wondering if it would stay afloat.

Yikes went the captain,
Crash went the glass,
In poured the water,
The captain knew he would not last.

'No!' went the crew
Glug went the boat,
The crew said their last goodbyes,
Totally taken aback.

Natasha Lavery (11)
St John Houghton Catholic School, Kirk Hallam

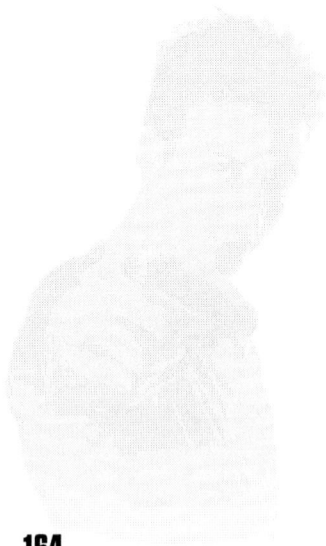

The Storm

Crash and bang through the night,
That gave me a little fright,
The thunder, clap, bang, crash,
It felt as though I was in war,
But even that would be a bore.
I couldn't sleep,
The storm made me peep,
And I even started to weep,
The noise it made,
It was so loud,
It felt as though I was in a crowd,
The light it made,
It would never fade,
The noise it made,
It was a rumble,
It made my belly jelly and tumble,
No one would speak,
They were too scared,
The storm could even last a week.

Joseph Cuomo (11)
St John Houghton Catholic School, Kirk Hallam

The Story Of The Storm

Drip, drop on the windowpane,
Drip, drop, the sound of rain.
Splish, splash as it hits the ground,
Splish, splash all around.

Crash, bang goes the thunder,
Crash, bang, where is it I wonder?
Flash, clash, I think it's lightning,
Flash, clash, it's very frightening.

Bash, boom, the thunder again,
Bash, boom, I'm wet with the rain.
Pssh, click, the window slides down,
Pssh, click all around.

Drip, drop, the rain seems to say,
Drip, drop, that's enough for today!

Jessica Gilhooly (11)
St John Houghton Catholic School, Kirk Hallam

Firework Show

Whoosh go the Roman candles high in the sky.
Crackle sounds the fireworks exploding above.
Swoosh spins the Catherine wheel spinning with delight.
Whoop praises the children as they see the fiery colours appear in the dark
of night.
Bang, bang goes the finale of the show.
Chatter, chatter go the people leaving the arena.
Silence echoes around Nottingham.

William Tooley (11)
St John Houghton Catholic School, Kirk Hallam

Jumping Into The Pool

Splash! Drip! Drip! Drip!
As I crash my way through the pool's defence.
Ha! Ha! Ha!
As the laughter of the children, laughing their heads off!
Aaaaaaaaarrrrrrrrggggggghhhhh!
As the children swim away from Monster Dad.
Thud! Thud! Scrape!
Is the fun of jumping into the pool.
Pat! Pat! as I get dry.
Tap! Thud! Creak! Bang!
As I shut the door behind me to go home.

Matthew Cragg (11)
St John Houghton Catholic School, Kirk Hallam

The Farm

Squelch, squelch
goes the mud.
Cluck, cluck
went the chickens.
Moo, moo, moo
go the cows.
Crunch, crunch.
Slurp, slash
as they eat the grass.
Oink, oink.
Splash, bubble
go the pigs in the muddy puddle.
Rustle, rumble
go the monkeys in the trees.

Imogen Wilkinson (11)
St John Houghton Catholic School, Kirk Hallam

The Hairdresser's

Ding-ding goes the bell on the door.
Squeak, squeak goes the leather chair.
Whoosh, whoosh goes the sit-down shower.
Drip, drip goes the wet hair.
Vroom goes the hairdryer.
Clip-clop go the customers' shoes.
Thump goes the customer sitting down.
Snip, snip go the scissors.
Snip, snip go the scissors.
Weesh, weesh goes the water spray.
Snip, snip go the scissors.
Ding-dong goes the bell on the door.
'Goodbye,' says the hairdresser.

Leah Wattam (11)
St John Houghton Catholic School, Kirk Hallam

Bang Went The Fireworks

Bang! went the fireworks!
Crackle! went the bonfire!
Swoosh! Swish! All night, all day.
Woof! went the dogs!
Fizz! went the sky!
Swoosh! Swish! All night, all day.
Tremble! went the cats!
Clap! went the fireworks!
Swoosh! Swish! All night, all day.
Screech! went the rockets!
Sizzle! went the glowsticks!
Swoosh! Swish! All night, all day.

Liam Hefford (11)
St John Houghton Catholic School, Kirk Hallam

The Farm

Whoosh went the wind,
Rustle went the trees as the wind whistled through,
Buzz said the bees as they raced through the trees,
Rumble went the tractor as it drove through the field,
Bark said the dog as he rounded up the sheep,
Baa said the sheep as they went through the gate,
Bang went the gate as it closed behind the sheep,
Cluck said the hens in the field next door,
Miaow said the cat,
Cuckoo said the bird,
Flutter went the bird's wings as it flew away from the cat,
Shuffle went the horse's hooves as she took a step back in surprise,
Moo said the cows in the field in front,
Sizzle goes the pan in the kitchen inside,
Zoom goes the plane overhead!

Millie Wheeldon (11)
St John Houghton Catholic School, Kirk Hallam

A Storm

Dripping, dropping, falling down
The wind swishing, swooshing
Frightening all the town.
I can hear the thunder
Rumble growl, snort
Now comes the crackle
The zip, zap caught.
Here it goes again
The terrifying rumbles
The fizzes, then whams
The wind as it mumbles.

Sarah Hutchby (11)
St John Houghton Catholic School, Kirk Hallam

A Test

Click of biros
Click, click, click, click

Zip of pencil cases
Up and down - zip, zip, zip, zip

Tick-tock of the clock
Tick-tock, tick-tock . . .

Gosh when will it stop?

Squeak of chairs against the polished floor
Squeak, squeak, squeak

Clip-clop of teacher's shoes walking around inspecting work
Clip-clop, clip-clop

Scribble of pens against paper
Scribble, scribble, scribble, scribble

How can I concentrate with all this racket?

'Test over,' booms Teacher's voice
I stare down at my paper
All there is . . .
A blank page

Thump goes my head against the desk!

Merrin Shelton (11)
St John Houghton Catholic School, Kirk Hallam

The End Of The Day

Tick!
Tick!
Goes the clocks.
Ring!
Ring!
Goes the bell.
Chatter!
Chatter!
Go the children.
Clack!
Clack!
Go the footsteps.
Honk!
Honk!
Go the buses.
Bang!
Bang!
Go the doors.

'Yay school is over!'
Scream the children.

Milla Rigby (11)
St John Houghton Catholic School, Kirk Hallam

Tiger

Tiger, tiger dying slowly
Tiger, tiger oh so lonely

Tiger, tiger fast asleep
Tiger, tiger dreams deep

Within 10 days, within 10 nights
Tiger, tiger was out of sight

In one corner of one dark hollow cage,
After all thoughts days of pain and rage. Shhh.
Tiger, tiger is left to sleep.

Sian Hooton (11)
St John Houghton Catholic School, Kirk Hallam

The Storm

Bang, crash, bang, I sat on my bed
Listening to the frightful noise outside.
Creak, creak went the bed as it shook.
Flash went a light through the curtain.
Boom went the thunder, I jumped under the cover.
It went quiet for a while,
I lay there shaking like a bobble head.
Bang! Crash! Bang! Creak! went my door
As my mum came to check on me.
But I was no longer in the bed.
My mother searched frantically
Then finally found me hiding under my bed.

Orlagh Condon (12)
St John Houghton Catholic School, Kirk Hallam

A Tap, Tap, Tapping

As I walk down the pitch-black lane,
I hear a familiar tapping,
It's followed me all the way here,
A tap, tap, tapping.
I try to walk lightly, trying to blend into the shadows,
I strain my ears and hear,
A pad, pad, padding.
I decide to sit down and completely stop,
Even though my heart's a thud, thud, thudding.
I strain my ears again and listen to the silence,
As I stand I walk lazily, heavily walking along,
There's no mistaking this time.
Plod, plod, plodding.
I suddenly have a brainwave,
I think I've worked it out,
I know the mysterious plonking,
I immediately know what to do.
I stamp my feet and gallop along,
Crash, bang, stamp, wallop, whack, bam,
Whish, shuffle, rumble, zoom.

Niamh Rogers (11)
St John Houghton Catholic School, Kirk Hallam

The Storm

Whoosh went the wind,
Tweet went the birds,
Zoom went the bikes
As the warden yelled, 'Yikes!'

Splash went the rain,
Squish went the rain,
As it hit the puddle,
Chirp went the birds,
As they started to huddle.

Boing went the hail,
As it hit the kerb,
Bark went the dog,
Nothing left, only mist and fog.

Ben Widdowson (11)
St John Houghton Catholic School, Kirk Hallam

A Stormy Night

Rat-tat-tat went the rain on my window sill.
Boom! went the thunder answering madly back to the lightning.
Crash, crash! We hear the lightning strike a tree.
Creak! Bang! The huge tree hits the ground.
Boom! Carries on as the thunder calls.
Crash, crash! We hear endlessly as the lightning strikes.
Thud, thud! I hear now as the hail hits my window sill.
Whoosh! goes the wind swirling around the house.
I hear people screech as they walk down the street their coats and hats fly off.
Splash, splash! I hear people run in puddles.
Trickle, trickle now goes the rain on my window sill.
There's nothing there anymore, all is silent.

Lucy Stanton-Lynch (12)
St John Houghton Catholic School, Kirk Hallam

The Big Race

Vroom!
Went the cars at a big pace.
Whistle!
Went the whistle because it was a false start.
Boo!
Went the crowd because they had to start again.
3, 2, 1, whistle to start the race.
Vroom, vroom!
Went the cars again.
'Hooray!'
Went the crowd that was supporting the winning racer.
Crash!
Went the car, it's over for him.
'Oh no!'
Went the crowd, but the race goes on.
Beep! Beep!
Went the car as it past the finish line.
'Whoo, oh yeah!'
Went the driver that won the race.

Oliver Ball (11)
St John Houghton Catholic School, Kirk Hallam

The Minibus

Bang! goes the door
Chitter-chatter, chitter-chatter
Brrr! goes the engine
The music blasts out
Everybody starts to sing
Creak! goes the door
Argh! goes everybody as they get out.

Lucy Parsons (11)
St John Houghton Catholic School, Kirk Hallam

My Poem

Alton Towers is bright pink,
Fun and exciting
I can taste the wind,
My mouth starts drying.

The fear of the fall,
So scary and frightening
The plunge through the tunnel,
So fast just like lightning.
The screams are so loud,
Your ears start crying
The sensation is great,
It feels like you're flying.

But then the seats stop,
Your knees begin shaking
The danger is off,
But your heart is still racing.

Emma Jelpke (14)
West Bridgford School, Nottingham

Messy Room

A rainforest of electrical wires.
Mountains of dirty clothes.
Fog clouds of dust.
A sea of rubbish.
This is my room.
And my room is like the Earth.
But more messy.

Savva Ermoyenous (14)
West Bridgford School, Nottingham

Pear

The rustling trees,
Which sent a shiver right to my knees.
The wind stood up and he did say,
'What can I do for you today?'
So I did say, 'Bring me a tray
Of fruit and veg, don't worry I'll pay
OK?'

So I journeyed on into the forest,
Where I met the local florist.
I said, 'Nice gloves you got there,'
He said, 'I know they're for picking a pear.'
'Wow that pear must taste good!'
'I know,' he said, 'It's really a spud.'

Calum McManus (14)
West Bridgford School, Nottingham

My Old Book

All covered in dust,
My career gone bust,
Help! Help! Get me out of this place
So people can see my hardback face.

'Ouch! How many pages ripped out?'
I said as I got thrown about,
Doodles and scribbles all over,
Got thrown out, surrounded by clover.

Amy MacLachlan (13)
West Bridgford School, Nottingham

Walking Along The Beach

A cool winter's day
Freezing fingers going blue
Hearing dogs barking
Chasing after waves

Smelling salt
When waves wild
Laughing, giggling, smiling
With the family

Sun shining
Wind blowing in your face
Hearing wave after wave
Crashing against the sand

Every day on a different beach
Walking along the sand
Peaceful, relaxing
Only without Dad.

Amy Buckingham (13)
West Bridgford School, Nottingham

Sandwiches

Sandwiches to eat,
For a school day treat.
One of strawberry jam
One of finest ham
And two tongue of ox
Packed in my lunch box.

Olivia Harker (13)
West Bridgford School, Nottingham

A Spring In His Step

Spring in his step,
down the street.
can you hear
the funky beat,
of the 'tap, pad, tap, pad'
of his one shoe off,
one shoe on
long, thin, marred skin,
belong in the bin
feet?

Shower? Never!
He would say, never accepting,
always deflecting,
no higher calling than to be with him,
kind, gentle, loving, lean,
words that embody him, but,
strangely,
never, ever, deniably clean . . .

Jack David Howells (13)
West Bridgford School, Nottingham

The Chocolate Fountain

I walked up to the chocolate fountain
I was dazzled by the sight.
I tasted it, my face lit up with delight and it was very nice.
Chocolate on my face, chocolate on the floor
and chocolate every place.

Sam Oldknow (13)
West Bridgford School, Nottingham

Waves

I step my feet into the sand,
And it's almost as white as snow.
I tried to grab a fish with my hand
And tried not to let go.

I like to eat a lot of tasty chips,
While looking at the tiny ships,
And here I smell the salty breeze,
While the sand is rubbing on my knees.

I can hear the waves crashing,
Oh wow it is smashing.

Edward Leckenby (13)
West Bridgford School, Nottingham

Night-Time In The Forest

The wind howled all around,
Through the trees, across the ground.
The leaves were dancing around the floor,
Each time faster than before.
The moon watched over the forest so dark,
The light reflecting off the bark.
All became quiet, peaceful and still,
In the forest, on the hill.

Brandon Aughton (13)
West Bridgford School, Nottingham

Asda

Frantic shoppers fill the aisles,
Harassed mother with screaming child,
Twenty minutes to do a full week's shop,
Coffee, teabags and fizzy pop.

Cage-like trolleys block the path,
These wobbly wheels are really naff,
Queues at the deli make my blood pressure high,
Two more minutes and I'll surely die.

Can't find the mustard for my pork pie,
Where's that . . . that shop assistant guy,
My bag for life is in the boot,
Guess the environment's down the chute.

James Riffat (13)
West Bridgford School, Nottingham

The Gnome

I went to the shop
I bought some pop
Full stop.

On my way home
I saw a gnome
Who had no home.

When I got home
I told my mum about the gnome
Who had no home.

So he stayed in my home.

Jacob Davies (12)
West Bridgford School, Nottingham

Rainforest

Motionless, I wait, like an ancient frieze,
hot humid air suffocates.
Mottled light moves in a breathless breeze
butterfly, flutters by,
lightly brushes a motionless flower
ants meander, daintily drawing a pattern
stillness, calm
jaguar swiftly moves into view,
shudders, shiver down the forest spine
walking with pride muscles bulging
he drags his nose across the floor, searching
freezes, frozen like a statue,
slashes his jaws crash below,
feathers fly,
birds die.

Sophie Cole (13)
West Bridgford School, Nottingham

Sam . . .

As I ran Sam ran
As I jumped Sam jumped
As I climbed Sam climbed
And as I sat Sam sat
Sometimes Sam walked in front
But mostly behind
Sam went everywhere with me except
At night, Sam had to go home
This is when I get lonely.

Sam . . . is . . .
My . . . shadow . . .
Forever . . .

Gideon Holmes (14)
West Bridgford School, Nottingham

Words

Words mean everything, but do nothing,
They can hurt, comfort or snitch.
Words tell stories,
Advertise and make you wonder
But still do nothing!
All they can do is make you think -
Bad, good or neither.
They're always there but you never notice them.
But they still do nothing!
When we talk they're only a tool
Just there in space
Words can mean all kinds of things;
Horrid, sad or happy.
But still do nothing!
Words can mean many things
Cold, red or death,
They can describe, manipulate and trick
Words can make you blue or green with envy.
But still do nothing!
Words are only ever there
If we want them to be.
They make things work
And help things advance
But still do nothing!

Words - only a tool for speech!

Nicky Holt (13)
West Bridgford School, Nottingham

I Have A Dog Named Blue

I have a dog named Blue
I tell him what to do
He obeys my every command
Will sit if I raise my hand

I have a dog named Blue
He always chews my shoe
He sometimes is a pain
When I have to walk in the rain

I have a dog named Blue
He has a high IQ
He's a clever dog indeed
He'll even fetch his lead

I have a dog named Blue
Without him I wouldn't know what to do
Always there with a wagging tail
Always there without fail

I have a dog named Blue
He's black and scruffy too
With a wet nose and two bright eyes
His happy spirit never dies

I have a dog named Blue
He gives me lots to do
I play with him all night and day
He just doesn't seem to go away

I have a dog named Blue
He is loyal, fun and loving too
He makes me laugh most every day
A friend for life he is here to stay.

I love my Blue.

Amelia Grout (13)
West Bridgford School, Nottingham

In Loving Memory

Even though I can't remember,
I still think of you at night
Especially on the 16th of September,
When I try to make it right.

I was only two years old,
When you left your heart of gold,
You went with not a word,
It was like no one heard.

So now, so peacefully you do remain,
But if only you could come back again,
You would fill the hearts of many lovers,
And even be such good friends of others.

You left a big mark in everyone's life,
Even your loving and caring wife.
So every day that we go on,
We have to think where you have gone.

It's not fair, why do we have to suffer?
With no father and only one mother.

So today you lie within the ground
And yet make not one sound.

I just want to say how much you are loved
And that I can't wait to meet you up above.

In loving memory of Peter Esden
16.9.47 - 23.8.99.

Emily Esden (13)
West Bridgford School, Nottingham

Haikus Of The Year

January
New year is dawning
Chilly start for everyone
The frosty winter.

February
Pancakes getting made
Red roses passed everywhere
Children eating lots.

March
It's St Patrick's day
Mothers cheerful as ever
Easter's kicking in.

April
Clocks going forward
Big Easter eggs are eaten
Watch out for the fools.

May
Summer's sneaking in
Bank holiday for people
Water fights are near.

June
Father's day today
Daddy's happy as ever
Wow! June already.

July
School's nearly over
Let's get ready for summer
Teachers get a rest.

August
Yeah! School is finished
Let's jet off on holiday
Six weeks of pure fun.

September
Autumn's coming near
It's the start of a new year
Oh no! Back to school.

October
Winter's creeping in
Scary time for everyone
Get out your pumpkins.

November
Guy Fawkes Day today
Fireworks are in the sky
We're all excited.

December
It's Christmas at last
Yes! It's now snowing this time
It's nearly New Year.

Gurmeet Landa (14)
West Bridgford School, Nottingham

The Second Half

Right now we need a goal and fast,
I hope our strikers are going to last,

They sprinted and shot for about the whole game,
Just to make this team look lame.

Just on 70 minutes we get our break,
Striker takes it like a piece of cake,
Now we're one up with 20 minutes to go,
And the whole team doesn't feel so low,
80 minutes gone we get another chance,
Now all the fans start to dance,
Now we're two up with 5 minutes to go,
Until the other team gets one back with a long throw,
Now we are winning and trying to defend,
I had a shot from 40 yards, what a bend,
What a goal for the club, I thought it was cool,
Until the whistle blew for the offside rule,
We are now top of the table, we did ascend,
And we won the match 2-1 in the end.

Joe Coleman (14)
West Bridgford School, Nottingham

Nottingham Forest Vs Derby County

Forest! Forest! Playing in red,
With their goalkeeper named Fred.
As they play against Derby at home,
At their ground called 'The Dome'.

The game kicks off at half-past three,
When they score they jump up and down with glee.
Derby gets a goal back,
So Forest need to get back on track.

In the second half Derby take the lead,
Paul Anderson running with speed.
The game is coming to an end,
So Derby starts to defend.

But Forest fight back,
And then they score against the Derby goalkeeper, Zak.
The match goes onto extra time,
Then the Derby fans committed a crime.

Forest eventually won this game,
Then they got all the fame.

Russell Caines (13)
West Bridgford School, Nottingham

31st Of October

Something is stirring on the night of Halloween
Evil demons and beasts and spider queens
You better watch out and try not to be seen
On this scary night of Halloween

Something is stirring on the night of Halloween
Late at night when the trick or treaters have been
The ghosts and ghoulies and evil fiends
Roam on this scary night of Halloween

Something is stirring on this night of Halloween
Houses are decorated in creepy theme
Pumpkins are carved and lit to look mean
Try not to be scared on this night of Halloween.

Michael Hinds (13)
West Bridgford School, Nottingham

The Seaside

The relentless waves crash onto the beach,
and grey pebbles litter the wet sand.
I smell the salty tang of damp seaweed,
and taste the bitter, fresh wind on the land.

The rocks are worn by ferocious waves,
their familiar shapes make the land.
The gritty sand digs into my feet,
as I hear a crab scuttle across the sand.

The familiar melody of an ice cream van,
brings me back to the here and now.
I rush to queue, the money in my hand,
for the best treat that I'm allowed . . .

Jed Sillitoe (14)
West Bridgford School, Nottingham

Tears

The clouds filled up, the rain poured down
My cheerful face turned to a frown
It travelled down the icy rocks
And spilled among the river docks

Down, down, down the water flowed
Beyond my cheeks right to my toes
It hit the ground, hard and cold,
Composure gone, it couldn't hold

Puffed up clouds from water spilled
Plunged to the grass and down the hills
Happiness drowned out of sight
I tried to stop with all my might

Muddy puddles clouded, brown
I couldn't see, my sight was drowned
Could such feelings come at ease?
Could happy feelings flow like breeze?

Melting, melting, breaking down
The raindrops won I slowly drowned
The tears sunk down right through my skin
Emotions raw I let them win

Battle ended, my defeat
Rain fought hard, the fight complete
My head was flooding with depression
Kettle brewed the tears had freshened

The clouds filled up, the rain poured down
What once was cheerful was a frown
It travelled down the icy rocks
And spilled among the river docks.

Anna Martin (13)
West Bridgford School, Nottingham

Mondays

Terror strikes
duty calls
to save the lives
before the tower falls

The clock is ticking
with no time to think
but only to react quickly
without a wink

People panic
people scream
they fear their worst
beyond any dream

They run with fear
and cry with shock
they all go running
in one giant flock

Over the bridges
through the streets
they ran in all directions
by the quickness of their feet

Their voices cried out
for help was heard
look here they come
all in a herd

The sirens rang loud
like one chilling scream
everyone knew . . .
what this would mean

Terror strikes
duty calls
to save the lives
before the tower falls.

Steven Swain (14)
West Bridgford School, Nottingham

Not A Morning Person

Mary is not a morning person,
She moans and groans and howls,
When she wakes, her breath does worsen,
And is needing to clear her bowels.

She always had bed head,
But constantly wants to snooze,
Always lies as stiff as lead,
But sleep she never seems to lose.

Her mum whips her curtains open wide,
Yet she doesn't seem to stir,
All Mary does is quickly hide,
Still nothing seems to occur.

Next her mum tries to lure her with chocolate,
But Mary continues to resist,
So after she gets her neighbour Ms Mocklate,
Who always seems to persist.

So her dad comes in with a giant horn,
And blows it with all his might,
She wishes she was never born,
And holds her covers tight.

Then her mum shouted, 'I'll make you pancakes for lunch!'
But after Mary said,
'It's now time for a late brunch . . .'
And her mum nodded her head.

So she drags her body out of her bed,
And dawdled down the stairs,
Like a baby she has to be fed,
But she's too tired to have any cares.

Mary is not a morning person,
She moans and groans and howls,
When she wakes, her breath does worsen,
And is needing to clear her bowels.

Frances Lamb (13)
West Bridgford School, Nottingham

Saw

The tale of Saw,
Is definitely not a bore,
This tale is a real thrill,
And will leave you in a suspended chill,
The blood and gore,
A story of true horror.
A hundred years ago on,
An island full of woe,
There was an old man,
And those who saw him ran.
The mask that he wore,
Would scare them away without a single roar,
They were right to run,
As he was worse than a gun.
A bullet to the head,
Would be nicer than his way of making you dead.
He was a dreaded curse,
No one knew of anything worse,
No one would ever say hooray.
But one day,
He came to his end,
His life hurtled off round a bend.
The life of this serial killer,
Ended in one last thriller.
He grabbed his blunt machete,
And picked his target a girl called Betty,
He found the girl,
She was as beautiful as a pearl,
He stabbed her in the neck,
Which left her a terrible wreck,
Her blood was spilt across the ground,
And her killer disappeared in a single bound.
The islanders said this was his last killing,
It would take everyone but they were all willing.
They ganged up around his home,
Ready to take him when he was alone.

They were armed with weapons of all kinds,
Each one in the glimmering sun shines,
The killer emerged from his house,
And the islanders attacked, killing everything even a mouse.

Now the island is home to Thorpe Park,
Where roller coaster addicts can have a lark,
But the ghost of the killer still roams around,
So if you feel a cold blade on your neck don't turn around!

Ben Barker (14)
West Bridgford School, Nottingham

Wacky Whales!

A whale is a fish
But 10x bigger
He eats with a digger
But ain't no singer.

He spurts out water
For a pestle and mortar
Rides a bike
'Cause he don't like trikes.

Tail like a fish
Mouth like a dish
Fins that flap
Jaws that clap.

Colour of the sky
But he don't like pie
Eats tons of krill
Voice is very shrill.

Knocks on your door
So you ignore
Until he starts to snore.

Kate Turney (14)
West Bridgford School, Nottingham

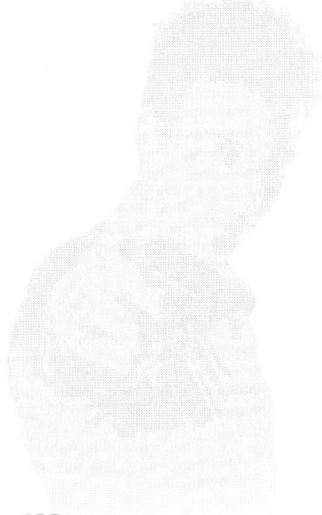

The Monster Hunter

Darkness was falling,
I could not see.

I was alone,
Just the darkness and me.

I was running home,
Wanting my supper.

Maybe father would make me
A nice warm cuppa.

Then he stepped out of the dark, dark shadows,
On his back, a bow and a quiver of arrows.

I gasped and took a step back,
Worried he might suddenly attack.

The smirk on his face was evil and mean,
I had thought I was alone but he was just unseen.

He drew his bow and aimed at my head,
Then, 'Duck,' he suddenly said.

He fired an arrow straight past my ear,
I turned and saw a monster that must have been near.

Green gunge was oozing from his brain,
I passed out, just realising this night had been insane.

As I feel the rain began to pour,
As my eyes closed, my mind felt raw.

Kieron Fisher (13)
West Bridgford School, Nottingham

Under The Bed

No one can have a bed as worse as this
Around the car is a mouldy sandwich
Which will make even the smelliest people sick
Near the back is my old toy
A robot which I named Sow

Then a plate that's not so bad
Then I realised it was mashed potato
A wet sock which smells like tomatoes
My old coats still damp as ever
And my old poem, I called never

Shirts which look so horrifying I cannot describe
Pens, books and even a dead rat
Which looks like it has gained so much fat
A toy plane, sunglasses and my underwear
And something from tech I think it's a t-square

Screwed up paper, oh who cares
A broken lamp, dusty and old
And something slimy that makes me go cold
O the bed is horrifying
O my god it's mine!

Habiba Shiekh (13)
West Bridgford School, Nottingham

Spooktastic Bats!

They sleep all day,
And fly all night.
If you're a moth,
You're in for a fright!

With long pointy ears,
And vampire fangs.
Upside down,
Is how it hangs.

The bat is the creature,
That insects fear.
It squeaks, then the sound,
Bounces back to its ear.

With leathery wings,
Which give it flight.
They're usually black,
But they do come in white.

Their swoop is so silent,
They attack from behind.
Pretty clever really,
Considering they're blind!

Bronwen Pole (12)
West Bridgford School, Nottingham

Dentist

Looking out the window in your car
Butterflies flutter as you realise you're not too far.
Then you think to yourself, *why so frightful?*
Just a check up, that's all
But in five minutes you'll have a mouthful
Of tools and all.
As your teeth get pulled and twisted
The man in the white mask makes you stay still as he insisted.
'Just some cold air now,' the man lies
And then the stinging pain makes you grasp your thighs.
He puts the tools down and turns away
And to my happiness that's where he chooses to stay.
I sit up in agony and grab my feet
But hold in my pain to show I'm not in defeat.
'All good,' the man says as my heart begins to lift
But drops back down again as he performs another twist.
As he brings out a clipboard and plots a date.
I know my day without a dentist, will have to wait.

Mark Webster [13]
West Bridgford School, Nottingham

The Café

The café is dark and damp,
and is only illuminated by a lamp.
The windows are shabby and unclean,
they once used to be delightful and pristine.

The buffet is disgusting and smelly,
not at all like the old little deli.
The trays are growing mould,
the tables are decrepit and old.

The café now stands where the deli once stood,
it was warm and inviting and everything good.
The food was always deliciously tasteful,
but the café that replaced it is hateful.

The café is dark and damp,
and is only illuminated by a lamp.
The windows are shabby and unclean,
where they once used to be delightfully pristine.

Daniel Greenhalgh (14)
West Bridgford School, Nottingham

My Bedroom

Last time I checked, my room was glistening clean,
But now there's food in the floor seam.

There are pants on the handle, fluffy dust on the candle
And there's even some rice in my sandal.

Jumpers all over the floor, socks swinging on the door,
Thinking about cleaning it, but it's such a chore.

I lifted up my old crusty quilt,
Only to find some milk that had spilt.

I sighed and thought, what should I do?
Noticing the bin which was full of tissue.

I walked a few metres, to look in the drawer
But slipped on a sandwich lying on the floor.

Cobwebs in the corners, dead flies on the sill
I'm sure I heard a mouse, which made me feel ill.

I saw the fan out the corner of my eye
Not noticing the wasp that was passing by.

I looked in my bag to find some school books
But all I found was two ice hockey pucks.

There was juice on the wall and crumbs in my bed
Not to mention what was where I'm supposed to put my head!

But of all the mess today I have found,
It's still my room and I always sleep sound!

Tyler Walker (14)
West Bridgford School, Nottingham

Shopping List

A pples, red and shiny
B ananas, yellow and plain
C arrots, orange and crunchy
D ates, brown and juicy
E ggs, white and smooth
F ish, pink and scaly
G rapes, green and bursting
H am, pink and wet
 I ce cream, colourful and cold
J am, red and tasty
K iwi, green and spongy
L emon, yellow and sour
M armite, brown and hard
O range, orange and sweet
P ickle, green and spiky
Q uail, whitey pink and feathery
R aisins, black and shrivelled
S oup, coloured and warm
T omatoes, red and healthy
U pside-down cake, coloured and creamy
V enison, red, brown and meaty
W heat, cream coloured and farmed
X ia, pink and shrivelled
Y oghurt, pink and milky
Z iti, yellow, white and curled.

Samuel Allen (13)
West Bridgford School, Nottingham

The Late Night

I hate my friends for keeping me out too late
I said, 'I got to be back to catch up with my old roommate'
I walk in the room to find my mate on the bed
But all I could see was that he was covered in red
My friends walked in and started to scream
I told them to be quiet and stop making a scene
I didn't know whether to leg it or sit by the bed
I was so scared of what the police would have said
It was too late the police were already here
My friend asked me what we were going to do
I said, 'I don't know my dear'
The police broke down the door to find we were gone
We never returned or I'd be hung!

Lahraib Hannah Iqbal (13)
West Bridgford School, Nottingham

Boxing

I threw my punches left and right, until he cried
but that's alright.
I threw my punches here and there, everywhere
but skimmed his hair.
I have my own phrase, and I like to be praised.
I like to win, and I like to put opponents into the bin.
I like to do my thing when people ask me I'll just say . . .
it was nothing.
I punch between the eyes
He flew right up to the skies.
I thought I had won because the bell had rung.
Instead another round had begun.
Brap!

Muaadh Shujahat & Arthur Oliver (12)
West Bridgford School, Nottingham

Monkey Tribe

In the days of young life,
As the monkey younglings strife.
The chief of the tribe
Hunts as he sends an angry vibe.
The chief goes down to the water bed
He sees an onyx by the water,
Waiting to be dead.

The Shaman gazes at the stars
And if she's lucky, sees great Mars.
The rituals are based in the depths of space
One is as the sun moves at a steady pace.

The forager leads to gather food,
Even if they're in a poor mood.

That's the story of evolution!

Jonathan Ewers (13)
West Bridgford School, Nottingham

The Seaside

As the waves crashed to the shore,
You're always left wanting more,
The sand gets between your toes,
And the smell of ice cream trickles past your nose,
You hear all the babies crying,
And see all the lifeguards spying,
As I'm putting on my suntan lotion,
I see the jet ski pros are going through the motions,
But then it's time to go,
And I asked my mum for my tenth ice cream,
So she said no!

Elliot Brown (13)
West Bridgford School, Nottingham

Forest

The wind howled over the trees.
It was a dark cold breeze.
I felt lost and naive.
The moon shone so very bright.
It left me with a fright.
The trees danced as the eerie wind blew.
The leaves just flew.
The branches twists and turns.
It made my stomach churn.
I miss you.
I don't know where to turn to.
Lost, alone with no home.
No one to hold my hand.
I think I may die.
Now I feel a sigh.

Aisha Mohammed (13)
West Bridgford School, Nottingham

Shadow

As the sun sets for another day
Nobody hears the endless cries
My life here seems to be running away
So many of us have broken ties.
Hate at night when all is quiet
A shadow lurking causing a riot.
It creeps closer and closer making itself not very clear,
My heart is beating at rapid speed, just out of fear.
It becomes apparent it's another one of me,
A lonely child not wanted by parents or society!
It creeps into my bed for what seems like all night
Longing for a love and a cuddle for free . . . shadow.

Ayesha Shah-Simmons (13)
West Bridgford School, Nottingham

My Brown Bear

My brown bear is furry, cuddly and soft
It is kept in my loft
Covered in cobwebs and dust
I need to clean it, I must
My brown bear

My brown bear has blue round eyes
He's got different coloured ties
He makes me smile
He's got style
My brown bear

My brown bear is old
His chain is made of gold
He'll always be my bear
Even if he does have a tear
My brown bear

My brown bear is always with me
Even for afternoon tea, see
A food stain around his lips
In his fur he has bits
My brown bear

My brown bear has earned a place
Not in my colourful case
On a shelf above my bed
Next to my other Ted
My brown bear

My brown bear is as clean as a whistle
No longer covered in thistle
His eyes are now squeaky clean
But his lips are still covered in bean
My brown bear oh I love you!

Amba Cooper (12)
West Bridgford School, Nottingham

Food Poem

Mmm food.
I have different types at different moods.
I like it on toast,
At the coast.
Don't have to boast.
Cos it's food.
And I'm in the mood.
For some cheese.
I like peas.
Lemon squeeze.
On your pancake.
Don't have to fake.
What you can't bake.
Cos it's food.
And I'm in the mood.

Tom Segal (12)
West Bridgford School, Nottingham

Cardboard Box

Maybe, you yeah you,
On the other side.
Could you just maybe put aside,
A little money,
Yes, money,
The stuff you waste away.

Maybe you can put a little bit aside,
In a charity today.
I'm not talking about the charity for kids and grandparents,
I'm talking about the one who clears the streets from them.

Yes them, them
I hear you scream.
The monster in the cardboard box,
No, no, no
The homeless, with nowhere else to stay.

Unlike you, they're there for life
With no husband, children or wife
You can leave home, move or stay
They are stuck with nowhere else to stay.

Maddy Flint-Foster [12]
West Bridgford School, Nottingham

Music

Music has a beat,
That makes you tap your feet,
Music makes you dance,
It puts you in a trance.

Music encourages you to sing along,
Even if you get all the words wrong.
At night when you try to sleep in your bed,
Remember the tune that's stuck in your head.

The speed of the song is the tempo,
That's whether it's fast or slow.
There are lots of words to describe a song,
But, is the duration short or long?

Music can make you emotional,
And it can even make you sociable,
Songs top the charts,
And even steal people's hearts.

This poem is coming to an end,
The finish is just around the bed,
But remember all poems aren't a bore,
Because this poem hasn't made you snore!

Emma Horne (12)
West Bridgford School, Nottingham

The Ballad Of Home

Home is all that I own
It's the greatest place in the world
I even have my own phone.

I have an electric drum kit
This is the best
I only play a bit.

All people there love me
I'm a king of my own house
And my subjects love me.

Home just feels perfect and right
The best place to be
When you're at home the future is bright.

My mum is a nurse
So me and my dad are safe
Home's the best place in the universe.

Freddie Ireland (12)
West Bridgford School, Nottingham

Reading Poem

Every time you open a book
You open a world of mystery
When thieves and crooks
Leap out of the pages
And commit a murderous crime

When one letter at a time
Create an image
Of the fantastic words
Their intriguing tales
Of mythical animals, never-ending trails

When people die
And others lie
Treason and plots occurs
The book is ending happily
With everyone crying heartily

May everyone hear me cry
Even up to the sky
That the book has finally ended
The plot of the story has bended
But oh how it feels so good
To have finally finished the book.

Hannah Simmons & Saad Ashraff (13)
West Bridgford School, Nottingham

The Nightmare

Running towards her like a slithering snake
Too late as she dies side to side
Tears dropping down her face
I held her hand and kissed her face
It wasn't the great time or place
My heart sliding out my chest
Her hair covering her face like a nest
No one stopped to help her out
Losing my voice as I shout
Her face was as cold as a block of ice
Is this real? Is this real?
I get on my knees beg and bleed
This is not real
I closed my eyes
I opened them
I lay there in my bed
Hugged my ted
What a nightmare!

Simran Purewal (13)
West Bridgford School, Nottingham

Night Sleep Tight

Before the children say goodnight
Have you screwed their heads on tight?
Mother father stop and think
Have you washed their ears with ink?

If a head should come unscrewed
Grateful case should be glued
Is you have failed
It should be nailed

Children's heads are very loose
Especially when they're not in use

Have you blinked the little ink?
I'll have to think and re sink
Oh Tony Blair don't you swear
Have a pear but just don't you glare.

Megan Smith (13)
West Bridgford School, Nottingham

A Trip Down Memory Lane

As I walked into the bare room,
I thought of all the good times,
Where we stood bride and groom,
And where we drank lots of wine,
With all the bottles in a line.

Now nothing's there,
Nothing remains of the time we shared,
And now my heart is broken,
But I doubt you ever cared,
Time to move on,
My husband is gone,
Never coming back.

Laura Dale (13)
West Bridgford School, Nottingham

The Internet

My computer's on I'm good to go,
Man! This connection is really slow.
I tell my dad we need a new router,
But he's just gone and bought my sis a new scooter,
They say Firefox is supposed to be fast,
For Heaven's sake it's just gone quarter past!
This computer's a load of slop,
Why didn't I buy that hi-tech laptop?
It's now half three, and I'm beginning to see,
Why people choose Macs over the PC,
Oh come on now, you're taking the Mick,
Hey PC, have you met my little friend the brick?
Right, that's it; we're going for a trip,
Yep that's right, back to the tip.

Andrew de Boer (13)
West Bridgford School, Nottingham

School!

School sometimes makes you a little bit stressed,
But at the weekends it's your time to rest.
When most of the teachers are really strict,
Don't put your hand up and you'll still get picked.
I wish that our school was cool and easy,
I wish the kids were nice and won't tease me.
5 days a week and you still get homework,
When in class we just talk about Dunkirk.
All of the school years have quickly gone by,
When I left Greythorn my mum had to cry.
Football at lunch is the best part all day,
However PE's not bad, I must say.
I suppose school isn't really that bad,
Just try not to make the teachers go mad!

Matthew Flannigan (13)
West Bridgford School, Nottingham

Kidnapped

I was walking back from the club late at night,
When suddenly a van came into my sight,
A man got out forced me in,
I saw his face, a scar deep within,
Locked in the back, I felt so dumb,
Why did I walk back without my mum?
After all that driving the car came to a stop,
The doors flew open with the sound of a pop,
The man dropped,
He has been popped,
With seconds of his life remaining,
Looked like my luck was gaining,
Saw a house, lights were on,
Walked in everyone had gone,
I sat on the floor,
And watched the door,
I had called my dad,
He had gone mad!

Ross Lory (13)
West Bridgford School, Nottingham

My Khaki Prince

She looked into her stone mirror,
Pictured him standing with her.
So far away her prince in khaki armour,
He promised nothing would harm her.
But when she thought of her prince she'd cry,
So scared that one day he might die.
Without him how would she stay alive?
She'd sit alone in front of the window, wishing,
That soon he'd be home.
The house was tall and scary;
She couldn't bear to be alone.
One day she got a mysterious letter,
She knew her life wasn't getting better.
All night she cried
Her prince had died.
No longer could she bear to breathe,
She decided she had to leave.
She could no longer live her life,
So grabbed a kitchen knife.

Lydia Fairhurst-Marshall (14)
West Bridgford School, Nottingham

My House

With my laptop on the table
My TV is big screen
Everybody loves it
In my living room with me

This is where I sleep
With a teddy staring at me
Everybody loves it
In my bedroom with me

This is where I wash my hands
And where I pee
Everybody hates it
In the toilet with me

This is where my meals are made
And my cup of tea
Everybody loves it
In my kitchen with me

This is where the flowers are
And my apple tree
Everybody loves it
In my garden with me

This is my house
It is owned by me
Everybody loves it
In my house with me.

Alex Fortescue (13)
West Bridgford School, Nottingham

Countdown To . . .

On TV, Countdown is about to start.
She sits in her leather brown chair
Sunlight shines through the window on her thin, grey hair
The cat sits purring gently where she lay
The only living creature she's seen in three whole days
One world war and eight decades she's seen . . .
So much life and fun she's been
She's got children and grandchildren - but they don't keep in touch
She has got friends, but they're old too,
So she doesn't see them much

Her fridge is stocked with microwave meals for one
Favourite is 'chicken-ding' because it doesn't take long.
What is she to do today? Bingo with the other old dears?
It's a way to socialise but she hates bingo and has done for years
Her withered hands still apply powder to her face
She's worn the same lipstick for forty years - Cerise Lace
She was a great beauty back in the day
Her husband would remind her - before he passed away.
If only people knew what her life once was
Would they patronise her like her carer does?
She was a secretary with shorthand and a good career
Long before the aches, the pains and the liver spots appeared.
She remembers the RAF dances during the war
The American officers knew she was the prettiest girl on the floor
Our Rita Hayworth! They said with a bow.
If they saw her swollen ankles, they wouldn't think that now.

I'm in God's waiting room, she thinks again
And she wonders how many episodes of Countdown until then
With a sigh, she slowly gets up from her seat
It's 'chicken-ding' for one - before Coronation Street.

Annabel Wakefield (13)
West Bridgford School, Nottingham

The Bag

Take out your books!
I did so
Reaching into my bag
I was greeted by a sock!
That smelt like a toe.

And an apple!
That made a crackle
When it touched my hand
An old worksheet
Crinkled and not neat

What's this?
A smelly old shoe
An old stick of glue?
This can't be my bag!

Oh wait . . . it is.

Joseph Ilett (13)
West Bridgford School, Nottingham

Looking At The Beach

I step onto the warm, white, luscious sand,
clutching a bucket and spade in my hand,
I feel the heat of the sun from a sky with no cloud,
noise from the car park is no longer loud,
the sun hits the calm waves with a glisten,
however it's not calm when I listen,
the smashing noise of an enormous wave,
is sure to put silence to its own grave,
and the trotting of people riding horse-back,
but the waves die down and the calmness is back,
there's a gentle swoosh of the long grass in dance,
so I stand and take a breath while I have a chance,
as I look out across the flat-sanded bay,
I think to myself what a dream day.

Georgina Jones (14)
West Bridgford School, Nottingham

One Day

The bricks and debris fly past my face,
I'd be anywhere, other than this place.
I sprint into the small building, running for my life,
To defend for close quarters, I take out my knife.
I turn the corner, with gun in hand,
I look down the sights of my M1 Garand.
An enemy sprints, down the corridor,
I gun him down, could there be any more?
I hear gunfire from far far away,
When could this all end, maybe today?
I reload, with a few bullets left,
I take some from a soldier, reduced to theft.
When suddenly, I hear a clang
A grenade explodes, making a bang
I am thrown back, off of my feet,
Today may be the day, when the Lord I meet.

I open my eyes and see a haze,
Rubble is everywhere, it seems like a maze.
I sit up and get out my colt,
I fire it, then the German stops to a halt.
He drops like a ragdoll, onto the ground,
His scream of pain, is a terrible sound
I stand back up and walk outside,
Our jeep passes by and I grab a ride.
We return back to our head-quarters,
Where they are firing off the mortars.

We rest, and then drive out to the trench,
The smell of dead bodies is an awful stench.
We push forward, to destroy the enemy tanks.
All I could see, was lifeless yanks.
The horror of war, served on a tray,
All of this, in only one day.

Alex Rudge (13)
West Bridgford School, Nottingham

My Grandma Bell

There is always someone in your life
who gives you strife,
in this case it's my grandma Bell
I feel like I'm in a cell.

I'm gonna try and describe her now
I think I know just how,
I really hope that you don't tell,
cos I will make you feel unwell.

She doesn't like meat
I think she smells of feet,
her hair looks like a pear
I hate her evil stare.

She can't walk right
I want to fight!
she is so slow
I just want her to go.

She can never hear me
I feel so teary,
she wears a brace
I always seem to get hit in the face!

She has bad taste
I don't want her to be replaced,
she can't even see me sometimes
so I can stay up past bedtimes.

Despite what I think
I don't want to blink,
and see her not there
I love her I swear!

Kirsty Witts (13)
West Bridgford School, Nottingham

When I Took My Friend Back Home

When I took my friend back home
She pointed out the garden gnome,
I told her if you think that's weird,
Wait till you see my dog's pink beard,
She chuckled but she didn't believe,
She had no idea what she would later receive.

As we walked up the zig zag path,
We heard the rhino in the bath,
I opened the door,
Revealing some more,
The monkey, the tiger, the goat, the pig,
All dressed up in my gran's red wig,
I only knew there was more to come,
Wait till she meets my fairy god mum.

She gasped a little and widened her eyes,
This must be one big surprise,
Just then flew in Henry the hen,
'Hens don't fly!' she shook her head,
Then jumped in my grandad Ted,
Dressed in a dress, with wellies and a hat,
'I bet you can't get crazier than that!'
I would later prove her very wrong,
But I gently pushed her further along,
The mouse, the owl, the bird, the worm,
And that dog with the crazy perm.
The little men danced from the next room,
I knew things were going to get crazier soon,
With orange faces and tiny feet,
My friend was in for a real treat!

'What's all this?' I heard her ask,
But out popped the flamingo wearing a mask,
I could tell by her face,
She was in disgrace,
Before I could explain,
It started to rain,
'How can it rain inside?' I heard her request,
'Must be a leak,' she must have guessed,
The zebra, the penguin, the cow, the kangaroo,
The chimpanzee wearing one random shoe.

The butterflies flying above our hair,
The pigs in the corner refused to share,
My fairy god mum walks in with a snake,
I can feel my friend starting to shake,
'Let's move on,' I suggest
I try to hide her from the rest,
But out comes Talking Tom the tiger,
Which really freaks her out,
So Talking Tom the tiger starts to fidget, growl and shout.

She ran out the door and slammed it behind,
Talking Tom the tiger said, 'That was unkind,'
I followed her out with the elephant and the cat,
She just said, 'What the heck was that?'

Kay Suzanne Ludlow (14)
West Bridgford School, Nottingham

Cosy Water

Cosy water
Line a scrawny smile
Of God's sunshine

Velvet hot,
Burns my wrecked skin,
Where my make-up stands -
Unharmed. Unprotected -
Lying across my mighty water.
A day after tomorrow,
I shall be gone,
To join my companion.

The stiffness of the wind
And the texture of the sun,
Alone.
My make-up floats,
And then sinks.
I am surrounded by my eternal friend,
Cosy water.
Which keeps me warm.

Mamoona Shiekh (13)
West Bridgford School, Nottingham

Animal Crackers

I walked into a field where I saw lots of sheep
as I looked around I noticed they were all on a heap.
They all stood there looking so proud,
but as I turned towards the bush something growled.
Out came a lion
who claimed that his name was Brian.
As I ran away I came to a house,
as I approached the doorway, I saw a mouse.

Through the doorway, down the stairs
looking around when I saw three bears.
Monkeys jumping on their back
coming towards me they were going to attack,
running to the toilet,
locking the door,
turning round to find a wild boar.
Washing his hair, back and feet,
outside the window I heard a tweet,
climbing through the window for my escape,
into the woods to face my fate.

Sophie Turner (13)
West Bridgford School, Nottingham

In The Silence Of The Night

As she steps on there is a slight crack,
Her face glistening in the moonlight,
Her feet glide, her body swirls,
She spins and she twirls,
In the silence of the night.

Her skates dig in hard,
As she dances on the ice,
She jumps, she dives,
Her body sparkles in the moonlight,
In the silence of the night.

Her lips ruby red,
Her fur coat wrapped round tight,
But she still shivers in the cold night,
She carries on to another clearing,
In the silence of the night.

But the ice is too thin,
It cracks as she swirls,
She plummets into the icy water,
She screams and she shouts,
But there is no one to help,
In the silence of the night.

Amy Robson (13)
West Bridgford School, Nottingham

It's A Rover

It's a Rover.
It was made in 1995.
But the guy behind the wheel was barely alive . . .
Literally
So we inherited it, cause it was in his will!
I love you Grandpa!
Anyway,
I can still remember that plate number.
HRW 505
And it's still running, in 2005!
And I ain't lying.
Apparently people are still buying.
But I don't know why.
All I know was that there was this guy.
He said it was worth a lot.
And we needed it cause there ain't that much that we got.
So we sold it.
And got quite a bit.
It's a Rover.
I hope it's treated with the respect that we gave it.

Samuel Taft (13)
West Bridgford School, Nottingham

The Monster

Be weary
This is scary
I walked into my room
With a really sharp broom
It was under my blanket
So I decided that I would shank it
Out came my AK47
And I sent it to Heaven
Its skin was blue
And it felt like glue
I felt glad
Cause the monster was bad.

Louis Salt (13)
West Bridgford School, Nottingham

Swimming

Front crawl, backstroke,
butterfly, breaststroke,
I swim them all,
it's not difficult.

25, 50, 100m
200, 300, 400m
I've swum them all
it's not difficult.

Diving in,
pushing off,
tumble turns,
I've done them all,
it's not difficult.

Pullboy, kickboard,
snorkel, flippers,
I've used them all,
it's not difficult.

So come on,
can you beat me?

Owen Morris (11)
Wilsthorpe Community School, Long Eaton

Funky, Funky, Zap, Zap, Zoom, Zoom!

Funky, funky, zap, zap, zoom, zoom
I like music, do you too?
I you do, do some funky moves
Funky, funky, zap, zap, zoom, zoom
I like dance, do you too?
If you do, do some funky moves
Funky, funky, zap, zap, zoom, zoom
I like darts, do you too?
If you do, do some funky moves.
Word!

Sam Armstrong (12)
Wilsthorpe Community School, Long Eaton

Autumn

Red, orange and brown leaves crunching under your feet
leaving the trees bare for their winter sleep.
Juicy fruits and nuts ready for eating while enjoying the last signs of
summer.

Animals of all kinds collecting nuts for the winter cold
while hibernating in their little holes with their furry friends.
Harvest is here and the crops are ready,
the corn brought in for the fresh bread.

The warm fire's on and everyone is ready for the hard winter's night,
Winter's nearly here but everyone's excited for who's coming
St Nicholas with his seven furry helpers.

Phoebe Buxton (11)
Wilsthorpe Community School, Long Eaton

What Matters To Me?

What matters to me?
There are lots of things that matter to me.
But I'll start with the sun.

When I wake up I rub my eyes and see the bright light
Then I gaze at the sparkly water droplets on the prickly fresh grass
I hear the robin tweeting at the top of Old Oaky
At the back of the garden.

What matters to me?

Laughter, I love hearing little kids laugh and giggle
They jump and jiggle a little.
I see the smiles on their faces
They scream and fidget when they get tickled

What matters to me?

My family, I love my cheeky brother,
He's always getting into trouble
And then there's my older sister trapped in
Her own little bubble
I have a little sister
She may be small but, a clever character

What matters to me?

World peace
Every child deserves to laugh and giggle
And put a smile on their faces and see the sun shine every morning
So let's not have war
Let's make world peace.

Munsanda Kasanyinga (11)
Wilsthorpe Community School, Long Eaton

Just Talk To Me

My life, family, friends, enemies
Whatever I've done wrong or right
I know that I've put up a massive fight
I just haven't heard from you in a while
But in the kitchen there's new tiles
But you don't know that because you haven't written back
to the letters that I sent
Just write back to me man
I know you probably hear this every day but I'm your no.1 fan
Please, I just want to hear from you man
It's been some time and we haven't spoken in a while
If you've not got the time
To write back on the flight back from Iraq
I was there man, you totally rocked the stand
I was waiting out there for 5 hours and you just blocked me out
You did that when I travelled to see you in your hometown
I've sent you my number
Please call me if you can
I've messed up my life and I just need some advice
Just for now I won't write to you
Until you write to me
Please, I need you, I'm dying trying to get things right man
You don't understand how much I want you to write to me now
This might be the last time I write to you so bye
You were my only ever idol.

Liam Burton (11)
Wilsthorpe Community School, Long Eaton

Clothes

I love clothes they matter to me
I wake up in the morning and nothing I see
Shall I wear a cardigan? Shall I wear a dress?
Give me ideas, I can't even guess.

Clothes to me, cost no fee
I just wish they grew on a tree
'Cause when I'm stuck
I wish I have luck
I think all my clothes are muck

But when I'm dressed
I just guessed
What to wear
Oh I swear
But in the end I look fine
I just think my clothes are alright.

Charly Cross (11)
Wilsthorpe Community School, Long Eaton

Chocolate

Chocolate is so delicious man
and now you can melt it in a frying pan
Go to the shop and someone took it
before you know it, it could be in a bucket
The Mars bars and the Crunchies too
and now they've even got Chunkies through
The chocolate chips and the awesome bit
and that in our jeans we can still fit!

Kieren Turner (12)
Wilsthorpe Community School, Long Eaton

My Life

I have a really big family
one that really cares
even when we have our
problems, the problems that we
share. We love to have our
family days out, think they're
really fun, we like to play
and mess about and chill
out when we are done
every other weekend I go to
see my dad, I go to see
other family, his pets
are really mad.
I love my family
as crazy as they
are, they mean
the world to
me, they
are the
best by
far.

Jade Dyer (12)
Wilsthorpe Community School, Long Eaton

Animals

Dolphins are playful, gliding through the sea,
Jumping over obstacles and swerving for their prey.

Sharks are evil, hiding in the sea and picking off their prey.

Turtles are wise, they know all the pathways
and return to the beach they escaped from.

Cheetahs are agile, moving with the wind,
working in teams to get the best prey.

Tigers are shy, they hide in all the shadows waiting to pounce.

We are death, killing all the animals that our
offspring deserve to see!

Isaac Olding (12)
Wilsthorpe Community School, Long Eaton

My Poem

I used to have a friend called Leon
He never used to rustle against his cage or make a sound
For he was my best friend before he drowned
He was always happy, I don't know what went wrong
Or how he went down that toilet
Now my poem is coming to an end
But I will never stop loving that parrot who was my best friend
Silence is roaming in my house
Now that Leon is gone.

Suraj Sharma (12)
Wilsthorpe Community School, Long Eaton

World Problems

The war is tearing the world apart.
We used to be the country everyone wanted to be.
We've got the Credit Crunch
We have fallen into a hole
Don't know where to go but
There's got to be a way to get out!
I feel sorry for homeless people
They've got no money or place to go.

Ryan Chadwick (12)
Wilsthorpe Community School, Long Eaton

My Friends

I hope my friends always have my back
If I go through a good or bad track
For example, my best friend Charlie Reeves
he's funny, he makes me laugh like a dummy.
Isaac, he's friendly
and he's not like a coyote
Charlie Crawford, he's kind
and not as mean as a bully.
Charlie Wilson, he can be crazy
So just back away if he goes a little wavy.

Alex Kidsley (12)
Wilsthorpe Community School, Long Eaton

What Matters To Me

What matters to me is my whole family
My brother might not be the best one
but in my heart he'll never ever be gone.
My dad will always harass me in a fun way
but again he will never go away.
My mum will always show me love
but let me tell you one thing Bruv
It's all 'bout . . .
Family.

Mario Christodoulou (12)
Wilsthorpe Community School, Long Eaton

The Music In Me

Music matters to me
A thing that makes me happy
Some people might like Aiden
Or even Iron Maiden.
I don't mean to boast,
But I prefer Slipknot most,
When I'm getting dressed
I put them on so I don't get depressed.
Blood is a great song,
But my sister thinks it's pong.
If you feel bad, put some music on
So you don't get too sad
The thing that matters to me,
Is seeing people really happy.

Ben Nequest (13)
Wilsthorpe Community School, Long Eaton

Sharks

We hear their name, it makes us shiver
A snap of the jaw like pulling the trigger
They eat meat like us but ten times bigger
They only kill for food
Rarely we're mistaken and chewed
But they're not to be messed with when in a bad mood
We go into their territory and make it our own
They see us as a threat and eat us to the bone
They can snap us up before we make a moan
But they're nothing short of beautiful
Even their size is plentiful
With grace they swim
With their arrow-like fin
They are often confused with danger
But they let us into their sea as a stranger
They get killed by hunter's nets
And no hope is given by our vets
All they want to do is swim
But their chance of survival is very slim
And this is what matters to me.

Jordan Gibbins (13)
Wilsthorpe Community School, Long Eaton

Before I Die

What matters to me is what I am going to do before I die

Before I die I want to be famous, rich,
I want my own show like Lilo and Stitch.

What matters to me is my future in university,
I want people to think more of me.

Before I die I want to fly in the sky,
I want to make my own lullaby.

What matters to me,
Is to be gifted like Bruce Lee.

Before I die I want to be a superstar,
I also want to meet Alan Carr.

What matters to me is to play at Wembley,
I want to sing in assembly.

Before I die I want a degree in maths,
I want my own town like Matlock Bath.

What matters to me is my family,
I want to live happily.

Before I die I want to live a nice life,
I also want a very nice wife.

Jake Rattan (13)
Wilsthorpe Community School, Long Eaton

What Matters To Me

What matters to me
is no racism
they just need to know
that if people are
different to you
in looks or
how they do something
they are still the same

If they can stop it in football
why can't we stop it now?

What matters to me is
I need to get good GCSEs
so I can get a decent job
and buy all the things I need.

Alex Sherwin (13)
Wilsthorpe Community School, Long Eaton

My Poem

What matters to me?
Dogs matter to me
they don't want to be in a cage all their life,
so get outside,
go adopt one or maybe two,
take good care of it, play with it
treat it like second nature,
like family or friend.
Don't just put it outside
when it gets too big or too much to handle,
they don't want to be left alone.
This is a living animal,
not a toy, treat them with care and respect.
What matters to me?
Dogs matter to me.

Tim Colley (13)
Wilsthorpe Community School, Long Eaton

Feelings

My life is getting confusing more and more
Decisions to make
People knocking on my door

My life is full of fear even more than before
Decisions to make
People knocking on my door

My life is full of happiness and sadness more and more
Decisions to make
People knocking on my door

My life is coming to me even more than before
Decisions to make
People knocking on my door

My parents fading more and more
Decisions to make
People knocking on my door

My life is mine once more
Decisions to make
People knocking on my door.

Joe Greenland (13)
Wilsthorpe Community School, Long Eaton

What Matters To Me

Why you matter to me
Your big, black eyes,
that shine like fireflies,
is what I like the most.

Your morning 'licks'
and good night flicks,
of your fluffy, long, white tail.

Your small, wet nose,
your furry face
which always cheers me up.

Your welcome home hugs,
that just warm me up,
when I arrive home from school.

The late night walks
we share,
as we walk from here to there.

You mean so much and
that's why you matter to me!

Dannielle Orrell (15)
Wilsthorpe Community School, Long Eaton

My Dog, Becks

Becks, you were wonderful in every single way.
I love how you ran up the stairs like an elephant charging
you were a star that was shining bright.
I still couldn't believe your hobbies were licking people's feet
faster than a cheetah
running for a piece of meat
and picking up shoes when someone walked in.
At least everyone loved you
apart from Lisa, when you picked up her shoes
why did you eat all the poos you could find?
But you were only a puppy
you didn't know better
at least you had a good life
just me and you.

Rory Donelan (12)
Wilsthorpe Community School, Long Eaton

Black Or White

Races, places different faces
People dark or light
Black or white
It doesn't matter if you're
Black or white
Just don't go round calling people
Black or white
Just come in together and let's unite
And don't be racist just because
Of different coloured faces.

Jessica Osei (12)
Wilsthorpe Community School, Long Eaton

Autumn

Leaves falling in the breeze of autumn
Like colourful rain
Red, yellow, green and gold
Enjoy it while it lasts
Children playing, laughing loud
Crunching leaves underfoot
Toasted marshmallows a welcome scent
Fireworks shooting to reach the stars
Autumn is an inviting season, which welcomes all.

Keziah Mather (12)
Wilsthorpe Community School, Long Eaton

Untitled

The reason I get out of bed
and ready every day
it makes me move, and sing, and shout
and get me on my way.

Without this thing I know and love
I don't know what I'd do
everyone in the world knows
that I'm nothing without you.

It might be strange and unlike me
to see me feel this way
but truthfully, from my heart
I'm glad that it's this way.

Love is the thing I need so much
without it I could die
and if I said I didn't care
then it would be a lie.

Kirsty Hartley (15)
Wilsthorpe Community School, Long Eaton

What Matters To Me?

Well what matters to me
is my horse!

Galloping, jumping, shows
everything that I do on
my horse and him of course.

When he jumps that's it
he's flying over like it's
1 metre 50.

He loves me
and I love him.

Galloping along that
lane is brilliant.
It's lovely, nice
and wonderful.
The feeling is breathtaking
I couldn't describe it.

On my horse that's
where dreams will
come true.

Someday, sometime
my dreams will
come true!
Me and Jack will
be there,
you just wait and see.

Long Eaton show
is where the
dreams begin.

Me and Jack will
get to my dreams.

We just have to
try harder to fulfil
my dream!

Sophie Hurst (12)
Wilsthorpe Community School, Long Eaton

What Matters To Me

What matters to me,
Is honest and true,
They are things that I love,
I don't know about you.

Books nice and thick,
With an engrossing story,
I prefer love and adventure,
Rather those which are gory.

To read in the shade,
Beneath the trees,
Sunlight all around,
And the occasional breeze.

To play the piano,
With its black and white key,
This is another thing,
Which matters to me.

It is not a tool,
But an extension of my hand,
We are the same,
Like how the shell becomes sand.

Family as well,
I love them so dear,
Some live far away,
But others live near.

Friends also,
With games and fun,
We work well together,
Like the rain and the sun.

Nature with creatures,
Plants and flowers,
But over its beauty,
Are fearsome powers.

With war and legends,
Comes history too,
But are all events,
Actually true?

With this we get mystery,
Learning and invention,
But there is one more thing,
I have yet to mention.

A thing,
That matters most to me,
Is doing just this,
Writing poetry.

Harriet Clark (14)
Wilsthorpe Community School, Long Eaton

Such A Small Little Thing

White and black
So soft and furry,
Such a small little thing.

Fast as a leopard
But as cute as a bunny
Such a small little thing.

As hungry as a bear
But as gentle as a hare
Such a small little thing.

As playful as a kitten
But as sleepy as a cat
Such a small little thing.

My little puppy, Skye
Is my little pie
I love her so much
Such a small little thing.

Charlotte Simpson (13)
Wilsthorpe Community School, Long Eaton

Untitled

I wake up, life is boring,
the feeling's constant every morning,
I feel my concentration, it's fading,
my education, degrading and it's blatant,
and you can read it from my papers.
My mind, developing emotional craters,
and the pain, in the back of my throat,
it's phasing, pounding like a migraine
and it's driving me crazy.

And I'm trying so hard to be sensible
but I'm close to the edge and I've tried to be gentle.
Don't tell me I'm falling cos I already know,
the pressure's building and my head's gonna blow
cos it's boggled out.
And all I hear them talk about - choices,
cut now I'm prepared for the fallout
cos these voices, chanting as I walk this plank
then go back to sleep,
not knowing what I just drank.

Ruben Symonds (15)
Wilsthorpe Community School, Long Eaton

Golf

In my hand I hold a ball,
White and dimpled, rather small,
Oh, how bland it does appear,
This harmless looking little sphere,

By his size I could not guess,
The awesome strength it does possess,
My life has not been quite the same,
Since I chose to play this game,

It rules my mind for hours on end,
A fortune it has made me spend,
It has made me curse and cry,
I hate myself and want to die,

I am promised a thing called a 'par'
If I can hit it straight and far,
To master such a tiny ball,
Should not be very hard at all,

It's made me whimper like a pup,
And swear that I will give it up,
And take to drink to ease my sorrow

But the ball knows
I'll be back . . . tomorrow.

Ben Pearson (12)
Wilsthorpe Community School, Long Eaton

My Life With My Dad . . .

The first time he held me it was like a dream come true,
I don't know what he was thinking but I think he felt the same way too.
He used to rock me in his arms like a rocking bird does,
when he hugged me I always got a buzz.
He used to take me to the park and push me on the swings
and when we used to play he sometimes used to sing.
'1, 2, 3,' he used to say before hide-and-seek,
he never used to play right because he always used to peek.
When we moved to Long Eaton it felt like a new life,
it was one hell of a journey but it was definitely worth the ride.
When we got there he took me to my new room,
and before we went to bed we lay down and stared at the moon.
He always used to make me dinner, a Sunday roast
and after that we always went to collect the post.
Time and time again we always had fun
then that one day, that day had finally come.
Even though he left it wasn't that bad
because sometimes we went to London to see him in his flat.
It wasn't so bad because we did have a laugh with him
we went to the park and sometimes went for a swim.
He always used to buy me stuff, especially fingers
and we used to listen to Kanye, 'Gold Digger'.
Then one day I came back from Kingswood and my mum sat me down
and all she saw was a big fat frown.

Jai Green (12)
Wilsthorpe Community School, Long Eaton

Heroes Of The Night

When you hear a noise at night
You might get a terrible fright
Your eyelids are low so you can't see
Now you need to find your dream key
Unlock all those mysteries
Forget about that scary sound
For it was the heroes of the night

They protect you when the world's at rest
That is their only quest
Forget those knights in shining armour
They're silly, untrusted and smell like a llama
They act as though they are the good guys
But it's actually you that they despise
Trust the ones unknown to Man
They live as a small, happy clan
They are the heroes of the night

They are not like superheroes on the television
They never make a wrong decision
They have no super powers, just abilities
They are the guardians over your cities
They don't want any glory
They are writing their own story
Now everyone is glad
And the knights are so sad
Because of the heroes of the night.

Rachael Wheatley (12)
Wilsthorpe Community School, Long Eaton

Food!

This is a poem I am dedicating to food,
I find it hard to believe it could ever be crude,

The sweet sort comes to thought,
With sour and sugary lollipops
That rot and dissolve your slobbery chops,

The salty sort comes to thought,
With salt and vinegar crisps to mind,
And nuts which squirrels like to find,

The greasy sort comes to thought,
With chips and kebabs oozing with fat,
And burgers that look like fried cow pats,

All this food is making me drool,
My book is like a mini pool,
Oh no, it's dripping onto Ronald,
I think I'll go out for a McDonald's!

Leila Rouse Bonnett (12)
Wilsthorpe Community School, Long Eaton

Untitled

What matters to me matters to a lot of people
An idol, a friend or a brother,
Also known as 'the rev'
An inspiration to thousands,
His memory still lives on,
And he could never be replaced

His death was felt by many
Loyal mourning fans,
A brilliant talented drummer,
His memory will never ever end,
And he will never be replaced.

Gabby Soar (15)
Wilsthorpe Community School, Long Eaton

Caution Llamas

Llamas are a docile creature
Long neck, playful, a beautiful feature
But when a car rushed down the road
100 miles per hour
Music overflowed
The llamas become stealthy, ready to fight
No hesitation to spit or to bite
You can run
You can hide
You can scurry back inside
But you are surrounded
And the llamas do mind.

Jack Sumpter (12)
Wilsthorpe Community School, Long Eaton

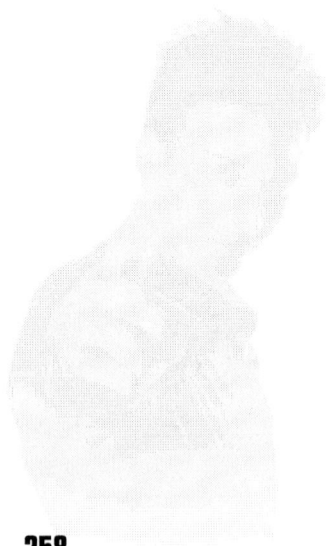

Young Writers Information

We hope you have enjoyed reading this book - and that you will continue to enjoy it in the coming years.

If you like reading and writing poetry drop us a line, or give us a call, and we'll send you a free information pack.

Alternatively if you would like to order further copies of this book or any of our other titles, then please give us a call or log onto our website at www.youngwriters.co.uk

Young Writers Information
Remus House
Coltsfoot Drive
Peterborough
PE2 9BF
(01733) 890066